Bon Jovi

Michael Heatley

OMNIBUS PRESS

London / New York / Sydney

Edited by Chris Charlesworth
Cover & Book designed by Hilite Design & Repro
Picture research by Nikki Russell

ISBN: 0.7119.6464.5
Order No: OP 47897

Exclusive Distributors
Book Sales Limited,
8/9 Frith Street,
London W1V 5TZ, UK.

Music Sales Corporation,
257 Park Avenue South,
New York, NY 10010, USA.

Music Sales Pty Limited,
120 Rothschild Avenue, Rosebery,
NSW 2018, Australia.

To the Music Trade only:
Music Sales Limited,
8/9, Frith Street,
London W1V 5TZ, UK.

Photo credits:
Front cover: LFI, Back cover: Bernhard
Kuhmstedt/Retna. All other pictures supplied by LFI
except Harry Goodwin: 20b; Rex Features: 16t

Every effort has been made to trace the copyright
holders of the photographs in this book but one or
two were unreachable. We would be grateful if the
photographers concerned would contact us.

Special thanks to Christine Heatley for research, Ian
Welch for advice and respect to major BJ guru Neil
Jeffries.

Printed in Great Britain by Page Brothers Ltd,
Norwich, Norfolk.

A catalogue record for this book is available from the
British Library.

5   INTRODUCTION

7   NEW JERSEY BOYHOOD

11   THE STRUGGLING YEARS

15   HEROES AND INFLUENCES

25   THE ALBUMS

37   THE SINGLES AND VIDEOS

45   HOLLYWOOD HIGHS

49   GIRLS, GIRLS, GIRLS

51   IMAGE

55   SOLO SCENES

59   BON JOVI WORLDWIDE – SHOWTIME

71   THE BROTHERHOOD

77   FAME – NO BED OF ROSES

91   HOMEWARD BOUND

95   FAITH IN THE FUTURE

Introduction

Before Bon Jovi came along, the dividing line between rock and pop was pretty well defined. Rock bands made albums, pop stars made singles. Rock, with apologies to Kiss and Alice Cooper, meant you were what you played, while pop often favoured style over substance.

Bon Jovi crossed that line, leading the way for a generation of bands to follow. They looked good, sounded good and in frontman Jon Bon Jovi they had the Italianate good looks that no teenage girl could resist. Ah yes, that was the key: while rock sold mainly to males, Bon Jovi's million-strong fan following crossed the gender divide like never before.

But what about the music? It's ranged from the airbrushed AOR of the first two albums to classic yet commercial peak of 1986's Slippery When Wet. After exploring different roads with Keep The Faith, they unleashed a Slippery... for the Nineties in These Days, a single-packed slice of hard rock with hooks.

There've been many false starts and skids on the road to fame. The break they took after touring themselves to death almost became a permanent split, while Jon's Hollywood ambitions and the departure of founder member Alec John Such both caused much grinding of the rumour mill. Yet they've stayed together like the New Jersey street gang Jon likes to think they are – and with guitarist Richie Sambora hitched to TV star Heather Locklear and drummer Tico Torres to supermodel Eva Herzigova they've found soulmates every bit as pretty as themselves!

Bon Jovi have lived over a decade in the media spotlight, and have never been short of something to say. Turn the page and hear their tale of Glory in their very own words.

New Jersey Boyhood

You know, if you ask me what the 1980s mean to me, it was when I grew up. To tell you the truth growing up's gonna take another couple of years for me, but I'm getting hints as to what that involves. I'm just getting to understand that at 27 I'm not a child. I'm having to become a man. It's not an easy thing to accept responsibility, and it's not easy to hang up your sneakers and think about being a grown man.   *Jon, January 1990*

Ever since I was seven years old I always dreamed of being in a rock'n'roll band. I couldn't play guitar then, but I remember I had a small toy guitar that my parents bought me for Christmas. Every day I'd come home from school and turn the Beatles on, just play along in front of the mirror making out I was them, and then I'd go out and play football like any other kid. I joined my first band when I was 15 and I met Jon when I was 22.   *Richie.*

The Beatles

I'm not an angry young man, and that probably works against me now, but I won't lie about it. I had nothing to be angry about then, I have nothing to be angry about now. It was a somewhat different time. When I was 16, there was the Bicentennial, the Yankees won the World Series, and in 1980 a movie star gets elected President and it's white picket fences and goes, 'Yeeeeah!' He convinced America to believe – silly as that sounds. I still believed the TV and the newspaper and the radio, and that may have got me where I am today.   *Jon, November 1994*

Pretty average, boring really. Both my parents had to work six days a week. My dad was a hairdresser, my mother did various jobs, but they had a hard work ethic. If they wanted something, they worked their asses off until they could get it so this was instilled in to us as kids, that you could get anything you wanted as long as you worked hard for it.   *Jon, January 1995*

I've always been a loner. In school. Growing up. I was never the life of the party. Never wanted to be.
                    Jon, February 1995

My first concert was Rush, Heart and the Doobie Brothers at a high school in 1975. It was overwhelming, I was only 13 at the time. By 1977 I was committed. I'd gone to a couple of shows and seen what it was all about. I'd seen

Bruce, I saw Southside Johnny and the Asbury Jukes in New Jersey, I saw Kiss at Madison Square Garden. I saw shows that were wild, but I never thought that I would be able to do it on that scale or go way beyond that. I wanted to be an Asbury Juke and they only headlined 3,000 seaters. – Jon, July 1995

I didn't have money to go to New York often. I went to jail once trying to go to a Bruce show there for selling posters outside. I'd go to the Great Adventure Amusement Park in Jersey to see the Michael Stanley Band, all those people making little records. By the time I was 16, I was sneaking into bars seeing bands on the way up like U2.
Jon, July 1995

Southside Johnny

Southside Johnny and the Asbury Dukes

The Rolling Stones

The Struggling Years

I was a gofer at Record Plant Studios. It was a real shitty job but I got to meet a lot of famous people which was pretty amazing. They were all really nice to me. It generally went the bigger the star the nicer the person.

I met the Stones. I was getting out of a cab, it was night time and we were scraping our money together to pay the cab fare. This was 1980, I'll tell you how I remember because John Lennon had just been shot and I'm paying off the cab driver and I looked up and just suddenly saw this Flash! Flash! Flash! Then I saw Mick Jagger and a couple of guys standing there looking pretty stunned because this photographer had just jumped out of this garbage can. Well two of my guys just jumped on the photographer and smashed him up against the wall and busted up his camera pretty bad.

Now Mick obviously knew this photographer but he still didn't want his picture taken but the photographer was still going, 'Mick, please let me have a picture of the Stones', so Mick put his arms around me and my guys and said, 'This is the new Rolling Stones', and called us the Fabulous Frogs or something and we had our pictures taken with him. I was 18 years old and blown away.

Jon, November 1987

The first time we got together as Bon Jovi it sounded like shit. You get everyone trying to do their own thing but there was definitely a feel there so we thought we'd persevere and see how it turned out. *Tico, November 1987*

A couple of the early gigs were terrible. We did one, and six girls turned up – no one else. Mind you, they screamed all the way through… and I think we might have even got an encore.

Alec, November 1987

We did another real bummer gig at Xanadu's in New Jersey on Thanksgiving Day. About 30 people turned up and there was a pole in front of the stage. And this isn't a well-known fact but there's this enzyme in a turkey called Tyagaline or some shit and it puts people to sleep: it's a relaxant, a pacifier. Anyway those people who came that night might have eaten some big turkeys because there were very few signs of life, man. That was without doubt our worst ever gig. Terrible. *Richie, November 1987*

David and I had been playing in various bar bands together since we were 16. We played all sorts of shit from R&B to Motown to kinda Aerosmith type stuff. Tico, Richie and Alec were playing in various bands on the circuit too. Tico had replaced Vinny 'Mad Dog' Lopez from the E-Street Band in a band called Lord Gunner and I'd seen him when I was about 16, so when we were getting Bon Jovi together and Alec suggested we get Tico in I thought, 'Great', despite having been pretty pissed off that he'd replaced Vinny Lopez. Richie was playing in a band that were doing real

well on the circuit and I was pretty impressed by his playing and his presence so I asked him to join.   *Jon, November 1987*

I put the band together in the first place because I'd had a kinda freak hit with 'Runaway' in '82 under my real name which is Jon Bongiovi. I didn't want to confuse everyone by saying that the band were called Jon Bongiovi so a guy at the record company suggested that we change the spelling around and the band all agreed. I went along with it and we became Bon Jovi.
Jon, November 1987

I worked in a junkyard, worked in a coupla fast-food joints, sold newspaper subscriptions door to door. That was like going to people and trying to persuade them that they need to buy a paper that doesn't even come from their town. Like, going round New Jersey and trying to tell people they need a paper from New York. I worked in a car wash for a short period, worked in a shoe store… all little jobs I couldn't hold down for very long. *Jon, August 1989*

Playing the local bar was the coolest thing in the world. Playing a college was the big time. I didn't even know where the continent of Europe was ten years ago – I would've paid a little more attention in school if I'd known what was gonna happen.
Jon, September 1990

To me in those days, Southside Johnny and the Asbury Jukes were The Beatles, because they had a tour bus! Then I remember the day we got our first tour bus – in January 1984 – and we rode on it to a gig in our hometown! We got in it at 4 o'clock in the afternoon, hung out there until midnight when we went onstage, and then jumped back on it straight after. Hey, sitting on a tour bus in the Holiday Inn parking lot… I'd made it! I was Mick Jagger that night!   *Jon, September 1990*

Dad taught me trumpet first; I took piano lessons at seven, and played rock and roll at 13. I still kept up with the classical – I just love music. And then I met Jon and we played in bands together.
David, November 1994

I was very focused; I knew there was nothing else in my life but this. Don't bore me with college or school, I will be making records. At that time, my only concerns were eating dinner and playing a bar and how was I gonna convince guys to play originals.
Jon, November 1994

I went on tour with Joe Cocker and that whole trip was a great learning experience because I discovered how record companies worked. How everyone has to do their job. That was when I said I can't do it alone. I needed another smart person, so when I met Jon…

First of all his charisma was outrageous. I went to see him play in a club in Jersey, and I walked in and I knew straight away… after I saw the show, I walked right up to him and introduced myself. I gave him a verbal resume, and said I had a lot of songs and I had a

Joe Cocker

knowledge of making records, and that their guitar player was very good, but he was very young. When you've got a bunch of mature musicians, they listen and complement themselves.

When you're young, you're just playing your bit and that's it. Jon was ready to make his run, he had it together already. He was charismatic, he was a great frontman. The band was kicking – and I was the missing piece. I really somehow saw it, and I never did anything like that in my life. I really walked straight up to Jon and went, 'I'm Richie Sambora, here I am, blah, blah, blah.'

Richie, November 1994

My main memory is of people throwing shit at us on our first big tour, which was opening for The Scorpions. But that's really the kind of thing that made us a strong band. What we basically learnt was if you stuck together you could beat anything.

Richie, November 1994

There's been a lot of innocence lost. I spent my early life on the road, I didn't have a lot of the reckless abandon when I was 18, 19. Most kids were out throwing up in the gutter and I was sitting at home practising, playing bars, writing songs, so by the time I was 20 I had a record deal.

Jon, January 1995

I slept on a pull-out couch – I couldn't even sleep on it – but my cousin let me stay there. And whenever he'd have women over, I'd have to go and sleep on the floor of this backroom without a bed because he didn't want me around then. And being turned down by every label. Working for 50 bucks a week. Not knowing anybody in town, so there'd be a lot of nights going to movies by myself. It was tough not knowing what your future was, for a couple of years there. But you live to tell. Many years later, I went back and called my cousin, on the Keep The Faith tour. We'd sold out a couple of nights at the Meadowlands and I hadn't seen him in ten years. I called him up on the way downtown. He didn't believe me. He said, 'Tell me my father's name.' I'm like, 'Tony, who the fuck are you talking to?' He says, 'You won't believe how many people have called up and said they're you over the years.'

Jon, February 1995

The first record sold 350,000. We thought that was cool because it's as many records as the Jukes sold and we got to go around the world and go to Europe, Japan and through America. I thought that was as big as it got, I didn't fathom the concept you could make money out of this. The first day we had a tour bus, we pulled into a bar and sat there all afternoon just because we had a bus, although we still lived with our mothers. Having a hotel room, wow! What a concept!

Jon, July 1995

Last time I gave blood was probably when I worked at a hospital, 20 years ago. My dad had a part-time job as the maintenance manager, so he got me the gig. I was just out of high school and I wanted to buy a Les Paul guitar, so I gave blood to get some money. I bled for rock and roll!

Richie, February 1996

Heroes and Influences

I met Bruce Springsteen in the studio... We'd met a few times and I'd played with him in the bars. I'd be playing with my band and he'd jump onstage and start singing with me. We'd sing old covers, old R&B songs and a coupla his songs. I still see him now, we played together not so long ago one night in Asbury Park, both bands on a stage no bigger than this room, in the Stone Pony.

Jon, November 1987

Bruce is to New Jersey like... I don't know how to compare it to something that you'd appreciate – but it's like the national soccer team! He's a sort of hero to the American public and he's a nice man, you know what I mean? He was nice to me when I was a kid. I first met him ten years ago and he helped me become who I am now, and you remember things like that when you're just a little kid. Now he's just a neighbour – we live in the same town, but we only see each other maybe two or three times a year. We move in different circles.

Jon, 1988

I'm truly excited about the chance to meet other musicians, because when you tour as much as we do, no other band is ever playing in town the same night! It's rare that another act is gonna be in town.

Jon, 1988

I've always admired Bono. He has a great voice. And I've been a real fan of U2 since the Boy album.

Jon, January 1989

Bruce Springsteen

Reggie Kray + prison warder

I'm infatuated with the Krays, I read their life story The Profession Of Violence. I even got Reg's autograph, the real Reg. It's on my wall. I've always been infatuated with crime.   *Jon, April 1989*

If mothers like Guns N'Roses, how radical is it? I read about Axl and it really surprised me, 'cos he has a lot of the same influences I have. He's the only other guy I've ever heard mention The Raspberries. That's about as pop as you can get.   *Jon, April 1989*

I listen to anything, I'm very broadminded. I like to educate myself. I always say I read records with my ears, and learn from that.   *Richie, May 1989*

I'd be lucky if I was half as cool for half as long as the Stones. That would be a good career though I'd like to go on as long. You know, I went to see the Stones this tour, eight years after seeing the last tour, eight years after walking out of the Meadowlands thinking, 'Wow, that was amazing.' So I went to Shea Stadium this year thinking, 'I can't wait to see the Stones, but am I gonna think differently because I could play this stadium now?' and I walked in there and I realised then Stones are still 50 times cooler than we've ever been… which is good because it gives you something to work for.   *Jon, December 1989*

It's funny because Bon Jovi and Def Leppard are really the same band you know. We're exactly the same characters from across different sides of the ocean. We got together and we're the best of friends. A great band – one of the best things to come out of England.   *Jon, 1989*

With Joe Elliot

Phill Lynott

Little Richard

Jesus! I loved Lizzy! I loved Lynott and his songs, but I never had a chance to see that band live 'cos they were never very popular in the States. In this world you need your friends and family to support you, and when people saw Phil going down the tubes, I just wish someone had grabbed him and said 'Hey, you need someone to talk to.' That's not an easy thing to do, telling someone that they have a problem. But for the sake of a brilliant musician and a human life is a great shame no-one sat him down.

Jon, January 1990

Little Richard's a legend's legend. When Richard walks into a room he looks like a star. You can't help but stare at the man. When he came into the place we were recording the record, everyone lost their minds. We all had our pictures taken with him. Jeff Beck got his autograph. When Richard walked in Jeff jumped up and stuck his hand out and said, 'I'm Jeff Beck and you're the reason I'm in this business.' Then he sat down and the emotion took over and he picked up his guitar and his fingers started playing 'Lucille'

Jon, January 1991

Jon with Bruce Springsteen

I get fucking sick of this Bruce thing… there's this great myth that we're always hanging out together but I hardly know the guy. The biggest mistake I made in my career was calling an album New Jersey, because suddenly everyone's comparing me to this guy. Making out that we're drinking buddies or something. We're not.   *Jon, January 1991*

Jambco is a great luxury that PolyGram gave me three years ago. If I want to release a record by anybody I like, I can. And if I don't want to, there's no big deal. I don't have to have a full staff. It's a boutique. It's the opportunity to put out a Billy Falcon I may stumble upon.
                                        Jon, September 1993

The only thing I dislike about Peal Jam is the hypocrisy. If Eddie Vedder doesn't want to be famous, he doesn't have to be. Don't do interviews! Don't release on Epic Records! Put it out on a small, underground label. So what? You can still express yourself and make great music!
                                        Jon, January 1994

Trent Reznor is someone I admire immensely, and yes, there's every possibility that there's now gonna be a wave of Nine Inch Nails soundalikes. But bands should do something with their influences and make the style their own.   *Jon, January 1994*

Trent Reznor

Kurt Cobain

Grunge is the voice of a disillusioned generation. I couldn't write those kinda lyrics, but Kurt Cobain did a fine job. What sucks are these record companies who smell money and sign 15 bands who look and sound the same. It invariably ends in disaster 'cos all these bands release one album and vanish.   *Jon, January 1994*

Music is a totally evolutionary process; there are people sitting in front of a computer screen making music that I get excited by – but the public don't understand how that happens. More than anything people have to see you play something to really understand it – and I thing rock'n'roll as a music form will be around for a long time, because there's an energy to it. There's that unspoken language, when your hair sticks up and you're singing and clapping and you're forgetting about your problems.
                                    David, November 1994

When I heard the organ with Deep Purple I went out and bought a Hammond. Then the American thing – I heard Roy Bittan with Springsteen – here's a classical guy who could play rock. Same with Wakeman. Then you listen to Zeppelin, and John Paul Jones is an amazing keyboard player, innovative. And Foreigner, 'Cold As Ice'. And The Beatles – look at the Mellotron, the flutes on 'Strawberry Fields'. You can use different sounds in different ways to really bring out something special.   *David, November 1994*

MTV were very supportive of the band in the late Eighties, and asked us if the band would perform on the MTV Awards. And discussing it, it seemed like every time we watched that show, through the little TV speaker, these huge bands would get out there and they'd sound like shit.

First of all, they're union mixers, and it's hard to do it on the fly, it's really quick. So Jon and I thought we'd showcase the song in a simple manner: we write on either acoustic guitar or piano anyway, so we decided to let the public in on the process...

It went so well, people were going crazy, saying how nice it was to see two guys get out there and not hide behind anything. We felt that showed we were real musicians and songwriters, to make the songs work that way. Then about a year and a half later, I remember reading Billboard and it was very nice to see they gave Jon and I credit for MTV deciding to do the Unplugged series. They gave us the credit, but they didn't give us any money.

Richie, November 1994

Heroes are important. What would we do without them? If there was no Bruce, there'd be no me – and if there were no Bob Dylan, there'd be no Bruce. If there was no Jimmy Page, there'd be no Richie Sambora.   *Jon, December 1994*

As far as melodic lead playing goes, I guess it's always got to my heart more. I love the nuances in other people's playing more than anything else – the little bends here and there, the subtle fills – and I guess it's how I approach it too. I've never approached a solo with that wanking kind of mentality – and that's with due respect to technical guitar players like Vai or Satriani 'cos there's a lot of talent there – but it doesn't fit the music I want to play.

Before I was in Bon Jovi, I was in a funk-jazz fusion band called Duke Williams & The Extremes and I got to wank profusely with them, ha ha! I was also in a progressive band called Message, so when I joined Bon Jovi it was different thing for me.   *Richie, December 1994*

Bob Dylan

To me, a good professional musician is always a good listener. That's the difference between a professional musician and an amateur. Knowing when to step out and when to step in is something I learned as a session player – I did my first session when I was about 18 or 19 in New York City. So it's important to be a good listener as well as a good player.   *Richie, December 1994*

Les Paul and I are really great friends. He's about 78 years old now but the guy still has all his faculties together. He's a great, great man and very intelligent. He's nocturnal and sleeps through the day but that means he'll call you at, like, three in the morning – 'Hiya son, how are ya?!' ha ha! I remember the time between Slippery… and New Jersey – we were desperately trying to prove to people that we weren't just a flash in the pan so we originally decided to record a double album. But we bit off a little more than we could chew and attempted to record about 28 songs. Now around song 17 or 18 I just ran out of things to do, I just went creatively blank!

So Les came over to my house on my birthday – he'd heard about my problem – and he gave me one of his Les Pauls as a present! It was a white one, I'm not sure what year, but he'd personally rewound the pickups on it and he said, 'Rich, take this guitar, go up to the studio and cut through that shit!' And it worked! So we became good friends.   *Richie, December 1994*

Richie with Les Paul and Skid Row's Snake

There are lots of great guitar players coming up right
now. On a personal level, I'd mention Nuno Bettencourt.
We toured with Extreme last year and I spent a great deal
of time watching him. He's very talented but he plays with
a lot of soul. On the grunge side I really like Soundgarden –
great guitar playing – Pearl Jam too; there's a band called
Stabbing Westward who I really like and there's Jeff
Buckley – son of the folk singer Tim Buckley – who's not so
much of a soloist but he has an amazing touch on guitar,
very fine.   *Richie, December 1994*

Costello, Waits and Dylan. Period. That's it. They are the
three greatest living lyricists in my eyes. *Jon, February 1995*

The E-Street Band had impeccable sound and I remember
the subtle qualities even more than any bombast. You
know, a song is truly magic when its singer and an acoustic
guitar can tell the tale. I guess for me Bruce's like my
Beatles, so of course it's a bit intimidating. On the other
hand, I guess that's why I can admit it because the music
and the band meant so much to me.   *Jon, April 1995*

My influences have been the modern day blues guys. Eric
Clapton has been a mentor of mine, and Jimmy Page. Jeff
Beck, of course, and Jimi Hendrix I have always looked up
to. I think that the style of guitar I play is not as flashy as
someone like Edward Van Halen's, who is a very modern
sounding player and obviously a legend. I play more rootsy
kind of style, shaped by the band's music because I learned
as a session player to play within the song and not try to
go round it.

Stevie Ray Vaughan

Recently I've got into Stevie Ray Vaughan. I don't know how I've missed him all these years, but a friend of mine gave me a tape of Stevie from 1985/86 and it was the most amazing guitar playing I'd heard. One day I think I'll have to do one of his songs as a tribute to him.

Richie, June 1995

Everything I still do live onstage is Southside Johnny Lyon. I told him that it's his fault I can't dance, because he never learned.

Jon, July 1995

We were blind to it. We certainly weren't listening to Nirvana or anything as an influence when we were recording Keep The Faith.

Jon on grunge and the new guard of music, June 1996

I did a painting of Jimi Hendrix and Miles Davis. I finished it about two days ago. I was in one of those moods, I was friends with Miles and a fan of both of them. They were geniuses. Miles was an incredible man. I met him playing in a jazz band around Harlem. He was also a painter. It was a matter of taste to sit in the same room as him sometimes, because it got intense, but I guess a lot of people didn't understand him too much. He was just a man; a great man and a very creative one.   *Tico, July 1996*

I do think I'm really, really good, but virtuosity can go too far. It's impossible to get a feel out of a 30 notes a second lick. Brrrrr! The normal person wants to be touched in the heart, not the brain. R&B is the art of space – in fact, that's the problem with classical music to me, it's all taken up by notes. Apart from a coupla sonatas which are nice, most of it's very notey.   *Richie, August 1996*

The Albums

After you do a lot of records together you're ready to try anything. Bon Jovi is a band that has always tried to make different records. If you look back between 7800 Fahrenheit and Slippery When Wet and then between New Jersey and the solo records, and between the solo records and Keep The Faith they are all stylistically very diverse. We always try as artists to grow, both the the benefit of ourselves and for the benefit of our fans, and of course by delving into new styles you've also got the chance of picking up new fans. *Richie, June 1995*

My lyrics are more socially conscious these days. They are the lyrics of a 33-year-old man. I'm not going to talk about the high school prom any more. I would like there to be a lot more sharing going on in the world. I wish that people were less judgemental and lot less self-centred and prejudiced, that we learn to live as one. That's what I'm writing about these days. *Jon, September 1995*

I started writing songs about the real world because I got older. When I was 25 and writing 'You Give Love A Bad Name', it was rock and roll fun. But when you're 33, you realise there's a big world out there. *Jon, November 1995*

Our album sleeves stink. All of them. We've never been good with sleeves. Tico is an artist, so maybe we'll get him to do the next one. *Jon, April 1996*

Bon Jovi

Our songs are about lust, not love. – Jon, in a 1984 press release to accompany the album

The first album was written from the point of view of five guys from New Jersey. The we toured the world and talked to the kids and saw who our audience was and saw what the band was. *Jon*

7800 Farenheit

You have your whole life to write your first album, and then you have six weeks to write the second one. When we made it, there were five of us sleeping together in a two-room apartment...

I liked that second album of ours, but when I listen to it now I can't justify why Lance Quinn, producer, did certain things on the production front, like multiple harmonies or doubling up the guitars at every opportunity.   *Jon*

Within the band and our label there was a feeling that 7800 Fahrenheit would be a massive seller, doing about five hit singles and selling in excess of three million albums in the US alone. But I was always more realistic... I said from the day it was released that I'd be happy if it went gold, and therefore I'm not despondent that we somehow failed to meet a specific target because to my mind things went well.   *Jon*

Slippery When Wet

It's just an absolute dream. I don't really think that any of it has sunk in yet. I mean 12 million worldwide is beyond anyone's expectations. Even in this country, I honestly

expected to sell one tenth of what we've sold here this year. I was looking at the sales of Southside Johnny and The Asbury Jukes who, for me, were the band and d'you know that their best-selling albums only sold in the region of 240,000? Even Bruce, who was Jesus Christ himself for me, only sold around one million copies of Born To Run, which was one the the best albums of all time, man.

Jon, November 1987

Oh man, all that sexist shit about the US sleeve of Slippery When Wet. Are you telling me that you'd rather have seen a guy in a wet T-shirt on the cover of that album? This ain't no faggot band, man.

Jon, November 1987

That was such a concise record, it just came out so easy, everything about making it was fun. It was very much destiny. We've made other great songs, other great records, but that was a special one. *Richie, November 1994*

New Jersey

The Slippery tour ended in Hawaii and we stayed there a while because everyone needed a rest. Then one by one we all left, apart from Richie who stayed there for about a month. We didn't do anything for three or four weeks then the phone calls started to change from 'Whatcha doing today?' to 'Hey, I got this next hook!' Then we demoed the first batch of songs. Seventeen in all. There was a couple of good ones in there but we really started to feel the pressure then because we didn't have the amazing song. I panicked, to be honest...

Richie was saying, 'Don't worry about it, we'll get back in the groove.' And I'm walking around the house yelling, 'I gotta pay for this place, we gotta write some fucking hot songs!' Then we started on the second batch and they came flooding out: 'Born To Be My Baby', 'Bad Medicine', 'Lay Your Hands On Me'... *Jon, January 1989*

I kinda think about things in a big way I guess, when I go for something I really go for it, do you know what I mean? But I like to think that a song like 'Blood On Blood' is more about friendship than romance. Anyway, who wants half measures? I like those kinda songs, always did. I love that majestic shit! *Jon, January 1989*

It wasn't meant to be a concept album. When our first record came out in '83 people didn't know whether we were from Italy or France or California. I wore a New Jersey patch on my back 'cos I didn't want anybody thinking I was from Hollywood. We decided to put a picture of that denim jacket with the patch on the album cover. The problem was they made it look like shit. New Jersey was the title of the album purely because I didn't want anybody to have any preconceived notions of it. That was as conceptual as I thought we should get at this point. *Jon, April 1989*

I think New Jersey is a better album. You improve as a songwriter through practice, and we've had plenty of that. We've performed live however many hundreds of times since writing Slippery so we've had that much more practice! New Jersey is a more diverse album, so hopefully it will make people realise that there's more to us than just pop. Obviously Jon's the pin-up, but there's no reason why he can't be a good songwriter too.   *Richie, May 1989*

Basically it's who and what we are and where we're from. It's an attitude that's summed up by the title, it's not conceptual. But you know, Jersey's still Jersey, it's our home and the people there have a particular attitude about them that they carry through life.   *Jon, August 1989*

Keep The Faith

Well, I tell you what, 'Women In Love' – I think – sucks. And I wrote it! I wish 'Little Bit Of Soul' wasn't on the record.   *Jon, September 1993*

As far as what's happening in the Nineties, I'm very pleased with how Keep The Faith has done. Quite frankly, I was scared it wouldn't do well. But it's exceeded my expectations – certainly over here in Europe. America is turning into such a trendy market that people are forgetting what's happened before. But the economic state of the nation has meant people can't afford to buy tons of records. We've done two million in the US, so that isn't bad. I just see the album as being a transitional one for us in the States, but it's opened up new, exciting market places for us abroad.   *Richie, 1993*

We'd spent six months on that record. We'd never spent six months on a record and I hope we never spend six months on another record. We were in five studios at one time come the end of that record. And I love that shit. I was running from studio to studio, everybody, doing something different, writing up to the last minute then finally saying, 'No, c'mon, we've gotta let it go.' But now, ten months later, I would change at least two tracks if not more. If only because there's another 20 sitting in my basement.

Jon, September 1993

Every time we do a single we remix it. We weren't in our right heads when the album was mixed. We recorded over 30 songs, and were gonna do a double album. That was a tall order, and by the end of it we were fatigued and ended up releasing just one album anyway.

Richie, February 1994

Cross Road – Best Of

It was very democratic, actually. We all got our secret ballots out – like, 'Nobody look! Nobody look!' But it was actually pretty easy; we didn't differ that much. Basically, we just looked at the reaction tracks, the songs that go down best with the people when we play live. There were a couple that were big hits – like 'Living In Sin' and 'Born To Be My Baby' – that didn't make the record because of songs like 'Never Say Goodbye', which I fought for emphatically, because I thought it was a song that said something. It was for the end of the record.

Jon and I would do that song live at the end of the show with just acoustic guitars and I would get sentimental and the crowd would get sentimental. It was kind of a message like, no matter what happens if you Bon Jovi fans never bought another record, I will always remember, this band will always remember, those particular times.

Richie, November 1994

How much significance is there in the title? Well, it is a transitional time for us... but then again Keep The Faith was a transitional time and album, so was Slippery When Wet, so were mine and Jon's solo records. I guess, as a band, we are at a crossroads right now. We're kind of starting anew, but it doesn't mean 'crisis' – people shouldn't read that into it!   *Richie, December 1994*

We wanted to put more songs on the greatest hits album – 18 songs – but that just wouldn't fit onto a single CD. We wanted to include my solo track 'Stranger In This Town', we wanted to put on 'Living In Sin', a couple of others, but it's a compromise. I reckon it's a good driving record – you put Cross Road on in your car when you've got to go someplace and it'll take you for a little ride also! It was kind of bold to put the new ones on and presume they'd be hits but... well, 'Always' has done okay for us.

Richie, December 1994

It's hard to say whether I have a single favourite of the hits. 'Wanted Dead Or Alive' I've always enjoyed as a guitar player and as a writer also. All those songs and riffs are from particular periods of time – they're like scrapbooks in my head. 'Lay Your Hands On Me' reminds me of one thing, 'Living On A Prayer' reminds me of another. I think that's what greatest hits albums are like, they kinda take me back to a certain time. As far as pure riffage I guess I'd have to say 'Living On A Prayer' – resurrecting the talk box was something, man! I think that worked out pretty good.

Richie, December 1994

The Greatest Hits wasn't planned. We were actually hoping to have this These Days record ready last year, but Jon and I took about 10 months actually writing it and so we were late starting to record it. The record company didn't want another instance like between New Jersey and Keep The Faith where there was a long lag time, and so they asked if they could release a Greatest Hits album to keep us in the public eye. We weren't too sure about that at all, because so often these things mark the end of a band's career, but we discussed it and realised we certainly have enough hits, and also it would be a fitting end to the first 10 years of the band.

But the reaction to this record has been amazing. We expected two or three million worldwide sales, but it's done about 11 and still going strong. We really can't believe it, we're as pleased as pie even now. As songwriters and as record makers it makes us real proud to have this kind of a reaction. And considering it wasn't our decision to put it out, we're overwhelmed and I'm sitting here smiling about it right now!   *Richie, June 1995*

These Days

There's a lot of inequality in American society that I can't alter and have had to come to terms with. I hope that this next album will reflect that far more than any previous Bon Jovi album.   *Jon, January 1994*

I still think 'You Give Love A Bad Name' is a great song, but there's gonna be nothing remotely like that on the new album. I've got things on my mind now that didn't bother me eight years ago, and I want to get them off my chest.   *Jon, January 1994*

It's obviously a lot closer to Keep The Faith than it is to Slippery… but it's different to anything we've done before.

Lyrically, it's way more introspective and the overall feel is a little darker.   *Jon, January 1994*

We've made our first batch of demos; 12 new songs. I don't know where it's gonna go directionally, but Jon and I have been very prolific. There's been no drought! We've got a lot of ideas, and the new stuff is very diverse. Hopefully, there'll be some more jamming on this record. And lots of guitar playing, which I particularly like! A very important part of our band is the live stuff, so we should get that on record too. We pulled it off well on the last album with 'Keep The Faith' and 'Dry County', so we'll hopefully have more of that this time.
                                              Richie, February 1994

You don't know exactly what to think about the first batch of demos, but I'm definitely excited by 'em! The thing is, with Keep The Faith, only one of the six singles was in the first batch. So that goes to show you where the first batch of demos usually is! I'm not sure whether we've got one, two or five singles, in the first batch, but the point is that there are some great songs and everyone's contributing.   *Jon, February 1994*

With Keep The Faith we were fishing for who we were; with this record I think we're more grounded, the band's very much back together again.   *Richie, December 1994*

From where I'm standing, this new album we're recording now is the best music we've written in a while so I'm very excited. But from a personal point of view as a guitar player I'd only say this – the guitar is an endless, endless road and no matter how far you think you've got, there's still a long journey ahead of you.   *Richie, December 1994*

After the last tour I went off to the Caribbean with my family to chill out. And that's when I started writing songs for the album! And before you know it, I'd invited Richie

out. So we ended up drinking a lot and writing a lot together. This was in January of '94, so it took 11 months of writing and rewriting before we ever demoed the songs. We started recording in Nashville but ended up trashing everything because I didn't like the guitar tones, the tuning, the keyboard parts. Then we came out here and started all over again...

Overall this record has taken 11 months to write, demo, make. A lotta time! *Jon, April 1995*

This was the first time that Jon and I have produced a Bon Jovi record per se, although we have produced in the past but not really taken credit for it. But this time around there was so much input from us on the production level that we decided to take credit for it. *Richie, June 1995*

People said These Days was so dark as a record. And I'm still trying to figure out why, because I was in such a good mood. With the new stuff, I'm writing a lot of humbling lyrics because that's where I'm at at the moment, between the kids and what I want to do with my future.
Jon, March 1996

These Days is probably the only record I like from top to bottom. I listened to it yesterday and I still like it.
Tico, July 1996

THE SINGLES AND VIDEOS

We play from the soul and the heart. I think we try to communicate with the fans more than a lot of bands do. Our music is communication, not masturbation! *Richie, May 1989*

I'm a fan of songs. So as a writer, it's difficult for me not to write hooks. I've never been much of a guitar player so I'm not able to write riffs as such. I never practised being Jeff Beck. I practised songwriting and that's what I get on with as soon as we come off the road.   *Jon, August 1989*

The song for me is like a screenplay, it has a middle, a beginning, and an end of course. Sometimes it starts with a riff, usually it starts with a title, and then Jon and I work on writing the blueprint of the song, and then bring that to the band and the band builds the house.
Richie, November 1994

It's like doing mini movie scores. You match the sounds to the story line – if it's a moody lyric you can't play happy eights. We painstakingly create those arrangements – we colour things and leave holes. When it sounds easy that means it's not…   *David, November 1994*

It was a real surprise that the first song we wrote together was such a good song. I remember first of all the three of us just sat down and we talked for a long time – a good hour and a half of conversation about who we were,

our theories of songwriting, which music we liked, what we didn't. And that's very important. What Jon and I usually do now is sit down over a coffee or whatever and just discuss what's on our minds that particular day.

Richie on writing with Jon and Desmond Child, November 1994

I enjoy working as a songwriter with other writers, because it's much more of a give and take thing – it's like, 'OK, I'll throw you the ball, you throw me the ball'. It's more like audience participation in a concert – the artist puts the energy out to the audience and the audience sends it back. It's a lot more fun to write with other people; when you write by yourself, it's a bit more tedious, you have to fight yourself. When you're with writers you respect... like the reason I think Jon and I are a good team is we debate with each other very healthily.

Richie, November 1994

After so many years, we know each other so well on a musical level – besides the friendship level – that it's a real comfortable thing. But there always seems to be some new stimulus somehow. I thing it's life experience, and also becoming a better musician. Every time you write a new song, hopefully – if you're paying attention – you learn the process, so you're actually learning to be a better songwriter. Just like every time you pick up a guitar the guitar becomes more comfortable to you.

Richie, November 1994

'Runaway'

The first video we ever made was for the single 'Runaway' in 1984. It's shit! Compared to the last video we did… well, it's like night and day. A disaster! A total embarrassment! You wanna embarrass me? Make me watch the video for 'Runaway' sometime!   *Jon, January 1990*

That first video was shot over a period of three days. We weren't even allowed at the shoot most of the time to see what the fuck was going on! It was done in a big old warehouse with some bullshit director who PolyGram Records brought in: he didn't have a clue. I remember our disappointment at seeing the video for the first time. We all drove up to our manager Doc McGhee's office in New York City to watch it. We were so excited. We saw it and afterwards there was just total silence. 'Trust us,' the powers that be said, 'It'll be great!' and all I could think of afterwards was the fact that they'd ruined my song – my life was over. It was really a question of back to the shoe store!   *Jon, January 1990*

'Living In Sin'

We finally did a conceptual video after not having done one for four-and-a-half years because the song just didn't lend itself to being performed live onstage. We spent a lot of effort and money on it and no one will take it… the English won't even sell it retail. They said it was sacrilegious and promoted teenage promiscuity and I told them that it was reality, but they didn't want to hear it. So it's been edited to death, unfortunately.   *Jon, December 1989*

'Bad Medicine'

Y'know, I hear all this stuff about simplistic lyrics. I personally like the lyrics a lot and people relate to them even if they're not exactly Elvis Costello. And it's funny, Elvis Costello has been quoted saying that his favourite song on the radio is 'Bad Medicine'.   *Jon, April 1989*

The chorus just appeared in my head one day – there were no instruments around us at all. I was with the band in Japan on the set of some commercial we were doing for Fuji tape or something, and it just popped into my head. I told Jon immediately and we worked it out there and then just with voices. So that's a kinda weird way to write a Number One song but as long as they keep coming to me I guess I'm not bothered how! I think that also shows that you can't polish bullshit – you got to have something that works in the rough if it's gonna work later in the studio.

Richie, December 1994

Sometimes a riff comes first, sometimes a melody to a chorus or verse will be first. In 'Bad Medicine' the whole melody and idea for that verse came to me on the roof of a hotel! But to actually finish 'Bad Medicine' after that riff took forever. Jon, Desmond Child and I wrote that, and it took five rewrites to get it all together.   *Richie, June 1995*

'You Give Love A Bad Name'

'You Give Love A Bad Name' was a title Desmond Child had. That was the first song we wrote with Desmond. After the second album, because we had a gold record and a platinum record, Jon and I wanted to get into the publishing and songwriting side – we wanted to be considered songwriters. So what we tried to do was go and write with a bunch of other people for their albums. And the funny thing with Desmond is Des came over for the first time and sat down and in about two and a half hours we had 'You Give Love A Bad Name'. And we said, 'We're not going to give this one away, we'll keep it ourselves'.

Richie, November 1994

'Living On A Prayer'

When I suggested the talk box they all looked at me like I was crazy. I pulled this thing out of a box from when I was 15 years old – at the time I was like 24, 25. I used to be in a band when I was a kid playing block dances in garages and schools, and at the time Frampton Comes Alive was very popular, so I was doing a lot of that, and Joe Walsh's 'Rocky Mountain Way'. I loved using that talk box, because it just caught people's ear. And it hadn't been really used for such a long time. I had this hook in my mind for 'Living On A Prayer'. When I started to do it, everybody laughed, and I said, 'Come on, man, just work with ma a little bit.' Then Bruce Fairbairn and Bob Rock producers both kind of liked the idea because it was quirky and different, and was going to add a new thing.   *Richie, November 1994*

'Living On A Prayer' was another weird one. I was working with a friend doing his record all the way through the night and we started drinking quite a bit of Jack Daniels and partaking of, er, anything else that was around. The next thing I know it's five or six in the morning and I was pretty fucked up. But I sat at the piano and started messing around with this chord change and it suddenly came to me. I went over to see Desmond Child and Jon and they were writing something that I didn't particularly care for, so I showed 'em my little chord change. And when they heard that everyone was out the blocks on that one – a hit!   *Richie, December 1994*

'Blood On Blood'

Reality, and yet it's fiction, 'cos the song's about the finer points of those characters and things that I'll never forget about those few years in my life, from however old you are in sixth grade, 12 or 13, until I was like 17. It's my own little

Jon and Dorothea Bon Jovi

movie. From 12 to 17 we were inseparable and we really experienced all the things of growing up together and maybe it's not as romantic, but in my mind it'll always be romantic. Beer to leather jackets to punk rock... I'll never forget about those years.

I saw Danny, who's in the song, a couple of years ago and I called him in March. I tracked him down. He lives in Florida. He's gained a ton of weight, he's going bald and he's funny, still as goofy as he ever was. I have no idea of Bobby. I haven't seen him in years. I heard he has two kids and he's married. I'd love to see him again. Dorothea was Bobby's girlfriend. There was the three of us, me, Danny and Bobby, and she was the girl. And then she sat next to me in history class and that was that. *Jon, September 1989*

'Keep The Faith'

The song, 'Keep The Faith', boy, I thought that was left-field for us: rhythmically, lyrically, the video and the look. And getting that kid Mike Edwards of Jesus Jones to do those dance mixes. We'd never even considered the idea of a dance mix before.   *Jon, September 1993*

'Always'

'Always' was written by Jon for a film called Romeo's Bleeding, and that's the first line of the song. We recorded it in England during the 'Keep The Faith' tour, but then Jon looked at the movie, didn't like it and so pulled the song. But Jon still liked the song so we went down to Nashville and re-recorded it for the album Cross Road.

Richie, June 1995

'Hey God'

I'm not going to candy coat anything anymore. A song like 'Hey God' questions things rather than just saying 'This sucks'. I will question authority and question myself, or the situation, to try and get the best of it rather than condemning it.   *Jon, March 1996*

I was riding in a limousine one winter day. We pulled up at a light and there was this homeless man on the pavement. We had eye contact. It was a serious moment. I felt very guilty. He was sitting in this cardboard box and I was in the back of a limousine. I thought, what the fuck can this guy be thinking of me? I thought in his head he had to writing a letter to God. God, what the fuck happened to me?   *Richie, August 1996*

'This Ain't A Love Song'

It's just us doing R&B. There's no deep lyrical meaning other than a 'broken hearts' song. A great, great singer with a voice better than mine could have a blast here! Otis Redding, for example. It's us flexing a little more of our influences.   *Jon, April 1995*

'These Days'

There's this line: 'The stars ain't outta reach but these days there ain't no ladder on the streets'. In essence, it's telling everyone that it's there to be had but it ain't easy. Nobody's gonna help you do anything, man, so forget all the excuses like, 'There's no ozone layer, there's no future, I can't get a job…' Of course it ain't right, but deal with it! I wanted to say in this song that there's nothing left but us these days. We don't have the white picket fences, we don't have any cheap excuses. Okay, fine! All we've got is us, so let's go   *Jon, April 1995*

'Something For The Pain'

The hardest song on the album. We re-wrote it 10 times! This song was meant to sound like T-Rex and it turns into something so incredibly unique that we can't even decide where it came from! A week ago, we finally finished the song after six months of toil! I came in with a new title, new lyrics, re-recorded the vocal.   *Jon, April 1995*

'Lie To Me'

Not only would it be a great hit but it'll be so cool to play live. It's Tommy and Gina growing up, saying, 'I can't make ends meet, but don't walk out on me 'cos I'm in deep shit. So if you can't tell me you love me, lie to me!' This didn't come from fiction!   *Jon, April 1995*

HOLLYWOOD HIGHS

Over the past few years, I've been sent script after script, but I've always turned them down adamantly. My singing career is not a step towards an acting career, and I'm still a believer of that. I don't wanna be Madonna and I'll never try to be a Madonna. For a start she's got bigger tits than me. *Jon, September 1990*

Just because you can sing and write songs doesn't automatically mean you're an actor. But what's worse is how many actors think they're singers, or even worse, songwriters. Makes you want to puke. *Jon, January 1991*

Well it's a hobby, I'm not going to quit my day job, as they say. It's fun, it's a challenge, and it's something I want to do more of. *Jon, September 1995*

It's still early days, you know? I'm just listening and watching all the time, just learning the trade. But it's certainly true that every time I do a movie, I feel a little bit more comfortable in that environment. A little more confident. I love movies, so I'm pursing my acting career with a real passion. But I'm not giving up on music. No way. Every day in LA that I wasn't on the set of Homegrown, I was in the studio, writing and recording new songs. *Jon, January 1996*

I read a lot of scripts, usually two or three a week, maybe more. I have an agency looking for me too, but they're only just beginning to realise what kind of things are right for me. I'm getting one or two film offers a week, but you have to choose what's right for you. It doesn't always have to be a big movie. I don't care if it's a small independent movie, so long as it's a cool script and I like the character. And I like the dialogue. You have to remember, there's a lot of shit out there. *Jon, January 1996*

I just watched Raging Bull again. It's amazing the physical transformation that he makes – you don't even see Bobby De Niro in that face. That's inspiring. I wouldn't be afraid of gaining 50 pounds or cutting my hair off or dyeing it blonde or blue. That would help me. *Jon, August 1996*

'Young Guns II'

It's just a short little nothing role, so please don't mistake this as the beginning of a great acting career...
Jon, September 1990

Oh it was just 30 seconds. I did a scene with the guy who wrote the thing, we escape from jail, grab the deputy, and then I get killed by the sheriff. It takes 10 times longer to explain it than it does to actually happen. It's become almost like a trivia question. Does Jon Bon Jovi actually appear in Young Guns II? My own grandmother went to see the movie and she said to me, 'It was very good but I didn't see you in it!' I'm in it and I'm not...   *Jon, January 1991*

You know you're in the movie business when you look in the mirror and you see yourself dressed as a cowboy standing next to Emilio Estevez.   *Jon, November 1994*

'Moonlight and Valentino'

There was a certain amount of secrecy involved because no one wants this movie to be perceived as mine. It isn't my film. I just have a featured role.   *Jon, January 1994*

It's just another outlet for me, just something for me to do while I'm not making records. It's certainly not a means for me to quit my day job. I just needed a hard-on this summer, and that was it!   *Jon, January 1994*

It's a real girls movie, you know, like Steel Magnolias. Filming was a great experience. It was real fun, and it should be out in April or May. I have a 'romantic interlude' with Elizabeth, but it's kinda like in the video with Cindy – just kissing. Which means I keep my pants on.
Jon, December 1994

Jon with Emilio Estevez

I wrote 'Letting You Go' for the movie I'll be in – Moonlight And Valentino. It'll surprise a few people! Dave Bryan's not playing on it, Hugh's not playing on it. It's just me, Richie, machines and a guy called Robbie Buchanan, a programmer. I was playing keyboards and singing it live; there's not vocal overdubs. I wrote the song as a gift. The only copy I had was on cassette and I wrote it for one of the movie's producers. It was a 'thank you' for having me. I didn't even want it in the movie, but they really wanted it in, so slowly it got there. I'm very happy with how it turned out.   *Jon, April 1995*

Jon With Liz Hurley
and Hugh Grant

The house painted in Valentino wasn't that much of stretch. I was just a nice, simple guy enjoying his life. Pretty much me.   *Jon, August 1996*

'Little City'

It's an ensemble piece about a bunch of thirtysomethings from San Francisco. Their lives are intertwined. You've got these six people who are desperately trying to figure out what life is all about and where it's taking them.

Jon, January 1996

'The Leading Man'

It's not full-frontal – I don't think that would get past the censors – but there is partial nudity. This is the first time I've done an intimate love scene.   *Jon, April 1996*

Jon with Demi Moore

I cut my hair because the movie called for it. Short hair does make me feel different, though. It doesn't feel like me. As soon as filming is over, I'll grow it again.

Jon, April 1996

I had my chest waxed and, I tell you, it was the most painful thing I've ever experienced. I will never, ever do it again! My chest bled and I screamed the place down. It was worse than having any tattoo done! It's the worst thing I've ever done. But it looks good on film.   *Jon, April 1996*

I got into amazing shape for that movie, and I'm losing that now. I said to everybody in the movie side of my life: 'You gotta understand something – as soon as I'm together with the band, it's all gonna go, because we drink every day. That's all we do – we lay in hotel rooms and drink.' When I'm focusing on the movie thing it's a whole different world. You live in the gym because there's nobody to play with. I'm falling apart now.   *Jon, July 1996*

I sat in my trailer, drank a lot of coffee and wrote songs. You know, it was the first time I was alone with myself in my whole life. No family, no band. I was with my wife from when I was 18 and I still lived with my parents then. Never had much chance to be alone. And look, I knocked out ten songs, the first batch for this next solo album. No tucking-the-kids-in-bed stories, I promise.

Jon, August 1996

This guy Robin Grange in The Leading Man is more of a chameleon's role. He's not exactly devious – it's more he tries to give people what they want from him. For instance, by fucking this other guy's wife.   *Jon, August 1996*

GIRLS, GIRLS, GIRLS

I had my share of fucking my way through Hollywood. There's nothing wrong with that. I had my share of that and I probably limited it because I could've had some more. But to tell you the truth I realised that wasn't for me.

Jon, December 1989

It all comes with age and experience. The times when all I wanted to do was chase women and get laid are over. Now I've seen so many other things.   *Jon, January 1994*

My tongue was certainly wagging that day! It was all in good fun, I swear! Cindy Crawford's a great kisser, she's a great... er... sport, and I still think the world not only of her, but also of Richard Gere. He's an immensely talented actor, and all I can say is that I'm sorry their marriage didn't work out. But I don't think a little kiss from me made any difference. My wife was very cool about it, too. She's been around me too long to worry about our relationship not being secure.   *Jon on a fun video shoot, December 1994*

I had some of those Anne Bancroft situations as a kid. When I think back to how rotten I was at sex then, I could kick myself. In retrospect it was fucking awful. Now, boy could I make up for lost time.   *Jon, May 1996*

Richie with wife
Heather Locklear

IMAGE

I've only got two tattoos — the steer's head and the Superman logo — but I want 20. I know I won't want the same 20 when I'm 60 so I hope I stop now. I don't think it hurts, especially on the shoulders. I find the needle, to quote John Cougar, hurts so good. It's fun. The adrenalin flows when you're getting it.   *Jon, April 1989*

I don't dress up no more. I'm not into that shit. I'm wearing these sunglasses because I've got the biggest black circles, man, under my eyes that you'd ever want to see. I feel like shit and look like shit and I don't give a shit. I'll tell you, if I was conscious about my image, I'd go back to getting that look that went up on all the little sisters' walls. I just stumbled on that look. My father cuts hair for a living so I've always had good haircuts. Then in 1986 the funniest thing happened, all these rock stars started having the same haircut. I'd be going, 'Hey, that's pretty wild, that guy looks exactly like me!' Then I thought, 'Fuck this,' and I let my hair grow all over my face!   *Jon, January 1991*

I don't know why my hair attracts attention. No, I don't like talking about my hair. Hair is hair. A man is a man! Who gives a shit?   *Jon, July 1993*

I learned early on that trying to be part of what's fashionable is a bad move. If I'd started out looking like Boy George and ended up looking like Eddie Vedder, I'd have some explaining to do! Back in 1985, all the LA bands were doing well and we weren't and for a minute we believed that what we needed was fancy clothes. Opening for Ratt every night, we became convinced that hairspray and lipstick were all we needed for massive success! Thank God we quickly came to our senses! If you just wear a T-shirt and a pair of Levi's and your record fails, at least you can go back to the bars knowing you never looked like your sister!   *Jon, January 1994*

It was easy to say after grunge that we'd become old-fashioned. But the last thing that I would do is start chasing fads and fashions. You always end up a dollar short and a day late.   *Jon, September 1994*

I'm a firm believer in a simple rule – a man can never have too many pairs of sunglasses or too many guitars!
                    Richie, December 1994

I hate all that stuff about the way I look. I can't believe all the fuss about my clothes and hair. I realise people say those things but I don't pay attention.   *Jon, January 1995*

I'm not vain enough to even think about whether or not I'm good-looking. I don't pay much attention to it. Yes there was a lot of attention when I got my hair cut but it was not big deal to me. I'm not Samson, I'm not gonna forget how to sing or write. I'm just not vain enough to think about these things. I've been wearing the same trousers for a week and I really don't care.

Jon, January 1995

I cut my hair two years ago. Like everything else in my life at that time, I wanted to change it all, so I took a lotta chances, got rid of the look and all the bullshit that went with that, just threw it away. I was bored. I needed a challenge. At that point I'd had a successful run through the Eighties and I wanted to shed excess baggage to move into the Nineties.   *Jon, January 1995*

I don't know why my hair keeps attracting attention. Maybe because my father cut hair for living but there's no threat of my cutting my hair off. No I don't like talking about my hair. It's a ridiculous question which has nothing to do with me or the band.   *Jon*

When I was a kid, people would say, 'What the fuck are you doin', man, making those faces?' It looked ugly, it wasn't sexy, the girls didn't dig it, all that. So I tried to stop. But I couldn't do it. I'd stand there for a while, keep my face blank. I was a fucking stiff! If I stop the facial expressions I stop the whole emotional flow from my body. So now I just say, 'Fuck you, man, this is what I do.' What happens is I'm playing lead, I'm singing in my head, but it's coming through my hands. So maybe my face is part of the whole trip.   *Richie, August 1996*

SOLO SCENES

The idea was that we'd go away for a couple of years, give everyone a break. Yet what with one project or another it seems as if we're drowning the market rather than leaving it alone! But I'm not gonna apologise for that because I'm a workaholic and I'll never slow down. I mean, right now I'm going through hell because I'm bored, and if another project came up tomorrow I'd probably do it.

Jon, September 1990

Man, I can't wait for people to hear what I've done. This isn't a Bon Jovi record at all, but rather one that allows me to take different turns and go all over the place. There's blues in here, R&B, rock'n'roll, some shit that BJ could never do. Of course, there are also points where I do deliver songs close to what Bon Jovi is all about. I'm just having so much fun on this record. *Richie, June 1991*

It's all over the place, man! There's a lot of different sides to this record. I'm a wild guy in my head and my imagination is gone! I'm exploring it with this record and I hope to make it a listening experience: When you put on the headphones, man, strap yourself in and check it out because it's going to be, like…woah! I'm thinking of putting listening instructions on the record, like – 'Turn out the lights, light a candle, lay down and let it take you.'
Richie, June 1991

The solo album 'Stranger…' gave me a lot of freshness in approaching my work within Bon Jovi. Doing a solo record you really find out about yourself because you have to wear so many hats it's a real push, but it's so rewarding. I'm very anxious to do it again – though not so anxious as to split the band for it. The band is more fun to be honest, and you get to share your stress and neurosis with four other guys.
Richie, December 1994

I don't know why, but I felt the need to do something for kids that are handicapped and can't always look out for themselves. Now that we've come to a convenient break in our schedule, it seemed an ideal time to release a single for the charity Special Olympics. And it turned out that Cindy Crawford was available and had agreed to be the love

Above and below,
Tico Torres with Eva Hertzigova

interest in the video. I said, 'I get to kiss Cindy Crawford for seven hours? Fine!'   *Jon, December 1994*

It's going to be the most modern record I've ever made. It's going to sound very different to the things I've done in the past. The whole approach to making it is different. There's all kinds of strange stuff on this record. Everything from trombones to kids' toys. I'd never written lyrics to an existing track before, and that was just one of the new things we did to keep the whole process as creative and spontaneous as possible. We'd mess around with all kinds of weird things. In a way, it's a very European-sounding record. Nothing at all was considered too 'out there'.
Jon on his new solo album, January 1996

Chris Evans invited me to be a quest DJ on his Radio 1 show, but someone from the immigration office was listening and decided that if I played records then I was working. And I didn't have a work permit! I wasn't even going to sit with Chris – I was supposed to stay on the other side of the controls. Not that I like DJing! It's just that Chris asked me and I thought why not?
Jon, April 1996

My paintings got noticed a couple of years ago. Eva Herzigova, aka Mrs Torres, spent hours sifting through things I had done over the years, and helped me set up a show in New York. About 400 people came and half the collection sold. I didn't know what to make of it. You've got your soul bared on all these pieces of canvas, and people inspecting it. It's a kick, but it's also very nerve-racking.   *Tico, June 1996*

I'm writing my second solo album like a horse right now. They're totally different animals, being in a band and doing a solo record. And I'm lucky enough to have both.
Richie, July 1996

I've written a handful of songs for Richie's new record. I put an instrumental record out, 'On A Full Moon', a year ago, and the Olympic committee love it and they're going to use it through the Atlanta Olympics. And I'm doing a new solo LP.   *David, July 1996*

This stuff is out of the realm of what Bon Jovi does, but right on the money as far as good songwriting goes. It's real guitar-orientated stuff. I want to get out of the thing where it's The Solo Album From The Guitar Player in Bon Jovi. Not that that's such a drag, but I want people to accept me as an artist in my own right, as a singer-songwriter and not just a guitar player.
Richie, October 1996

BON JOVI WORLDWIDE — SHOWTIME

A big show is a great cure for a hangover. You ain't feeling too good before the show but you get up there and sweat all that shit out of your system and you feel great afterwards and it's like, 'Awwlride! Let's go out and get wasted again!'   *Alec, November 1987*

We used to get a hell of a lot of knickers thrown, but we're playing that side down right now. I'm trying to grease my hair back and I'm not wearing any outlandish stage gear anymore.   *Jon, November 1987*

I think about this a lot and I end up thinking some pretty weird shit about what I'd do to make that two hours onstage as perfect as it can be. For me to give everything to those two hours I'd give up two hours of my life. That's pretty sick but it's that important to me. I'd kill to put on a good show because it means more to me than anything else in the world, friends, family everything. How's that for fucked up?   *Jon, November 1987*

I'm getting to be a cocky sonofabitch on this thing, aren't I? But I get scared every time – you bet I do. Flying without a safety net, man, you fall down and it's all over. You hold onto this thing and your knuckles are white and you're thinking 'Jesus, why am I doing this, please God don't let me fall'. But it's a neat thing, people are really surprised by it and they smile, and so it's a pleasure to do it for that reason.

Jon, on flying over the audience during 'Living On A Prayer'.

We never play the same. If you taped it every night you'd hear stuff that has to be the same, but we're always just changing things around. That's the excitement of it all. And the spontaneity between all of us – the eye contact – somebody does something which drives somebody else.

David, November 1994

It'd be so fucking boring to do everything on the record verbatim. When you're doing 150 shows or more, if you don't keep it fresh for yourself, you get bored and so will the crowd. I keep my playing different every night. There's a skeleton that I have to do to please the audience, but I'll always throw my own little new things in there. For me, that's lifeblood. Pop music is very tightly structured. Fuck that! That's why I play the blues all the time – there is no structure!

Richie, February 1995

I'm not nervous before I go on, man. I take the mental position that there's no question that I know how to do this. I jut go out there and do the one thing that I know I can do as well as anybody. It's not a cockiness but if I lose the confidence, if I ever look down from the tightrope, I'll fall. With all this heat I tell myself I'm sick, I'm sick, I'm sick. I go don't tell yourself you're sick or you're going to really fucking drown.

When the house lights go out, I don't change. I never felt that I became a character, even if it was a good, bad or an indifferent one, I never felt that I went out there and became 'him'. You don't take time to enjoy the adulation. You go out there and go, 'All right, this is as good as it gets in Bangkok. You got it, let's go.' You can't do it half-assed.

Jon, July 1995

You'll never see the same show. I change the set nightly. Unlike most people's jobs where they go to the same office for their whole life, my job is never the same twice; that keeps it fresh.

Jon, July 1995

I like stadiums. Some people say it's not personal but those are the guys who can't play stadiums. Stadiums are a real fucking blast. They can be as personal as you want them to be. I'll talk to the guy in the hundredth row; if I see him, I'll go, 'You with the Marlboro, what are you doing?' That's the magic.

Jon, July 1995

There's a ritual to going to a gig. As goofy as it sounds, the superstition of it all is actually the difference between having a great show and not. An hour before, you warm up and you figure out what the set's gonna be. That one hour is really regimented.

Jon, July 1996

We didn't want it to be one of those take-the-money-and-run tours. We said, 'Let's spend the money on the show and give something back to the people.' It's the most amazing thing I've ever seen. With this tour we wanted to do something that people wouldn't forget. It's a way of saying thanks and a way of saying, 'See ya'. The idea is to make it the most unique show we can, and to give the people everything they want to hear.

Jon on the summer 1996 European Tour, July 1996

It's probably the best-looking outdoor stage I've ever seen in my life, from anybody. From Pink Floyd to the Rolling Stones. It blew me away.

Richie on the summer 1996 European Tour, July 1996

We used to request a lot of booze, but it was slowly killing us, so now we don't drink as much during or before the show. We save the partying for later.   *Richie, July 1996*

It was an amazing day. It was one of the first shows in my life when I could say that we were on our way to becoming something. If you could lick that crowd, at the hour of the day we went on... In my house I have a picture of the five of us standing like this arms raised in triumph in front of this vast sea of people. It was great. We went on after Metallica, and they're always a kick-ass band. It's not like competition, but you just got to be as good as you can.

Richie on Donington 1985, June 1996

ON THE ROAD

I hated it towards the end of the last tour. I was tired and I loved going out there but I hated it. It almost killed me and didn't realise because you just run on adrenalin. There's time changes and you don't know what country you're in or what day it is and it really got to me. I look at the pictures that were taken then and realise how sick I was.   *Jon, January 1989*

I got a fractured leg. I cracked the tibia and I get it taped up so I can still bounce around on it. Maybe they'll have to cut the leg off, but only after the tour!   *Jon, April 1989*

I love festivals… hanging out with different bands, them watching you gets you up, and you watching them gets them up and in turn the kids get a great show, so festivals are always a blast.   *Jon, 1989*

It's an older crowd now than it was in '86. But what was cool was that they had been telling some younger kids, but, certainly, the bulk of our crowd had grown up with us through the years.   *Jon, September 1993*

Believe me the other 22 hours of my day suck! The last thing I want to do is travel around. I would love to get up on stage for two hours every day, then hit the Star Trek transporter and go home. People say, 'Where are you going on your vacation?' and I go, 'Home!'   *Jon, September 1993*

After the burn-out, I walked away and came back fresh and said, 'Ah jeez, this ain't so bad. I can do this.' So I handle the whole thing a lot better. I wasn't sick, run down or angry, throwing temper tantrums. I was having a great time, and when I wasn't having a great time I said I'd go home. Because there's no reason for us to do this unless we're having fun and that's what we're doing again, thank God!   *Jon, September 1993*

There's nothing I like more than a challenge. Onstage it's a challenge, 'cos you either suck or you win. We'll win all the time, even if it does fucking kill us! You only need to look at some of the bands we used to open up for – bands who are now completely gone. There are a lot of factors as to why we've survived, but I guess the main thing is that we've all managed to get along for 10 years!   *David, 1993*

I'm telling you this tour has been great – absolutely nothing like the New Jersey tour. All I wanted to do after that one was stay at home and not do anything. After I fell off my motorcycle and cracked my collar bone, I didn't have any choice!   *Alec, 1993*

We've managed to step away from everything and just look at what we've achieved. I still can't believe that we've played in so many countries to so many people, and sold millions of records.   *Richie, 1993*

This leg of the tour is sorta what we've worked for all of our lives – playing these huge outdoor venues every night. You almost feel like going out and shaking everybody's hand and saying 'Thanks!'   *Jon, 1993*

I loved it when we played there before. I thought Donington was great too, but I just feel that Milton Keynes is a great arena for music.   *Tico, 1993*

I kinda roll with the situations. I had more fun on the Keep The Faith tour than I ever had in the past. The abrupt, rocket-ship lift-off of Slippery… didn't wear off until the end of the New Jersey tour. Hardly until the beginning of Keep The Faith! It's been a trip coming to terms with being in a new place in my life. Finally, after a bunch o' years, we're comfortable with who we are. So if you ask me if I wish I was back in 1987, then no. I had a great time, but it was a blur. We didn't spend life on Earth! The reason the last tour was great, was that I remember most of it.   *Richie, February 1994*

There was a three year period at the end of the Eighties when we were never home. We toured our asses off – 16 months tour, 37 different countries, five nights a week at least. We were the most successful band on the planet for those three years, and we all knew how lucky and grateful and happy we were to be in the position. But we were so overworked we didn't even know it ourselves. We almost lost a couple of the band members – rock'n'roll is a very dangerous business, it can take your feet out from under you before you know it.

We had to take a break, and everybody had to get well mentally. It did almost get you. We realised we could not run at that pace any longer. We thought we could do it and survive mentally and physically, but it broke us down to the point where we were all very severely burnt out. Now what we do is carry a trainer with us. This was actually Tico's idea, which was a very good idea. Our last tour was a year, which is actually a pretty frightening thing, to be away from home for such a long time, but we decided instead of depleting ourselves with the drugs and alcohol and all the other stuff we used to do, now the best thing to do is actually at the end of a tour, get yourself in shape and work out so you're very strong. You actually enjoy the playing part of it more. *Richie, November 1994*

I go to a lot of shows, I'm still a big fan and I try to go and see everybody. But there's a certain feeling at our own shows which not a lot of other bands really get. It's partly because of the songs and it's partly because Jon is such a magical kind of frontman. The guy knows how to make a big place seem very intimate. *Richie, November 1994*

I did a bit of reflecting at the end of the last tour. We were in an airport van one day, and Troy, who was shooting the 'I'll Sleep When I'm Dead' video, said, 'Do you realise that you guys have been doing this for 10 years?' The guys said, 'And you didn't even buy us flowers.' *Jon, November 1994*

I missed the fucking last eight months of the *Slippery When Wet* tour because I was totally physically and mentally blitzed. But then, after I thought about it, I guess it's still the biggest thing that ever happened to me. A real once in a lifetime thing. Hopefully it'll happen again some day, just that whole experience of, you, know, the responsibility of playing all over the world in so many places and just touring our asses off. And also, trying to have fun at the same time and all that shit. It almost drove us crazy too. *Richie, November 1994*

Yeah, 22 hours a day can suck sometimes, but when it's time to go out there, that's why you went through all the bullshit – that's what you've been waiting for all day. *David, November 1994*

We're no longer doing any huge tours. When *Slippery When Wet* became a hit in 1986, we did two 18 month tours back-to-back and burned out so badly we didn't even speak to each other anymore. We lost the togetherness. We have learnt the hard way how to balance career and personal life.   *Jon, September 1995*

We've been in places like Peru, for instance, where the show was booked, but then the American Embassy asked us why in God's name we were coming! So we didn't play. It wasn't for the safety of me or the band, but God forbid if a crew member got hurt. I couldn't have the responsibility to them or their families.   *Jon, November 1995*

Basically we're just a touring machine and we're playing anywhere that's got a stadium big enough. We're just gearing up out here on a Far Eastern and Asian tour before we get to Europe. We started in Bombay, India, we went through the Philippines, through Indonesia and Kuala Lumpur, Singapore, Bangkok, where we filmed a video – we've been working! Now it's three stadiums in Japan, then we go to Milan and start our European tour in Italy.   *Richie, June 1995*

Bon Jovi always try and give a really good package first and foremost. All the tickets were sold before any support acts were announced so that's a tribute to us. Basically we just want to give people their money's worth, so as well as Van Halen we've got Slash with us on some dates, then The Pretenders and loads of others.   *Richie, June 1995*

I do drink too much, but what am I supposed to do? I'm on the road. I've got nothing to do. I sit around all day, bored out of my mind, waiting for the show.

Jon, May 1996

Yep. The knees, ankles, throat all start to go. I feel like I've been beaten beyond any semblance of sanity and brain power. I haven't got a brain cell working.

Jon at the end of a 105-date tour, May 1996

Being on the road is fantasy camp. And I know what it's like to go off the road and to start pacing the hallway in your house because it's showtime. Or when it's three in the morning and you're the only one up in your house and you're sitting by the TV with a bottle of wine because there's nobody who wants a drink with you. *Jon, July 1996*

I'm a fan when I go to a rock show. I want to see those bands play the songs I loved when I was growing up. And yet I'm an artist, and you want to play the songs that move you currently. So you're torn, but you're also there to satisfy the people that came to see you. They didn't hear you sing these songs 200 times. They might be hearing it for the first time. *Jon, July 1996*

I usually work with watercolours when I'm on the road. I can carry 24-inch canvases in a flightcase. I have about 120 pieces for my exhibition in England. *Tico, July 1996*

Tico and Eva Hertzigova at Tico's exhibition.

Billy Joel, Elton John, Jon Bon
Jovi and Sting

ROCKIN' RUSSIA

You know, at this stage of the game, it's like you ask
yourself, what can we do that Zeppelin or the Stones or
The Beatles didn't already do? And being here is it. Not
only do we get to come over in a good cause, we also get
to put on the kind of rock show never before seen in the
Soviet Union.   *Jon on the Moscow Peace Festival/*
Make A Difference Foundation concerts, September 1989

It's Bon Jovi going where no man has gone before. New
Jersey will be released there at the end of August and that
will be the first contemporary Western rock album released
in Russia. And this is official, it's not the black market. The
state-owned Melodia Records label is releasing New Jersey.
No Beatles, no Stones, just us.   *Jon 1989*

The Make A Difference Foundation deals with drug,
alcohol and substance abuse. The Russians have a problem
with alcohol over there, and it was a way the Russian
government would sanction the show, actually let it
happen. Even though Billy Joel went in there, Elton John
and a few other bands, no one's ever done it on this scale,
so the government have to have a reason to endorse it.
This show was initially gonna be just a show in America or
something, and now it's turned into the biggest show in
Russia.   *Jon, 1989*

I think that Glasnost and Perestroika are the future, thank God. From Gorbachev on is the future. There are all these drastic changes; they're accepting the finer points of capitalism. Making money for their people, opening up to the West, letting all the finer things that the world knows about in, is gonna save their country. It's still a long way from all the excesses that we have. Over there, if you have a tee-shirt to give away, you can buy more with it than you can with the dollar or any amount of roubles.

Jon, September 1989

I see Russia opening up and I can see why they're opening. There's this country where the military defences are the best in the world, but they can't build a fucking food blender. They've realised that when they built those walls around themselves they cut off their learning processes too. The rest of the world has passed them by and they can't feed their own people because there's not money there.

Money makes the world go round and the Russians have realised that, so they're gonna tumble those walls to make some. They're gonna open the gates and everyone's gonna leave and the West'll move in there! Then the Russians'll move back because there'll be a McDonald's built there with a job for them, so they can at least make some money. The West is just dying to get in there and rip these people off! Pure Capitalism! They've found out that Communism is a nice theory but it's shitty in practice! *Jon, January 1990*

I love going around the world and seeing all kinds of different people. Being an American, I was taught in school that the Russians were the enemy. Big time. And then we went to Russia and I went, 'Wow, they look just like me!'

David, July 1996

THE BROTHERHOOD

I've always said that if it was over today we'd still all go on vacation together. That's the best way I can describe it. We're like brothers.   *Jon, January 1989*

It started with The Sun newspaper in England and spread worldwide. The magic of Bon Jovi is the five guys in it, and it wouldn't make any sense for me to break up the band. I'll get around to Bon Jovi again when I get around to it. But I'm so busy doing other things just now.
                    Jon on rumours of a split, June 1990

We were at the end of the New Jersey tour in Mexico and I'm reading all this crap that Tico my drummer had quit and I'm looking for drummers. Suddenly I'm getting all these drummer tapes with photos and letters saying, I'm a hot drummer and I'm better looking than Tico. So I'm throwing all this stuff out the fifteenth floor of the hotel and I'm saying, 'Tico, you cocksucker, you stupid bastard, what's happening man? I'm reading that you've quit the band.' He doesn't know the first thing about it. He's been on a binge in Mexico and thinks he can speak Spanish.

Then we're off the road and I'm seeing the headlines 'It's All Over For Bon Jovi' – now Richie is quitting the band because we're supposed to have had some big bust up. I haven't seen the guy for months! But it starts shit up between you. That's the English press and, man, the English press is powerful because that shit goes world fucking wide.   *Jon, January 1991*

Listen, I love those guys more than my own family. We've struggled through some shit together. We're brothers, closer than brothers.   *Jon, January 1991*

I certainly never mentioned leaving the band, although I did say 'If Jon wants to break up the band, that's OK'. But even if he had done, I think he would have said 'C'mon – let's get back together.'   *Richie, June 1991*

I think Jonny was just really tired at that point – we all were man. I was begging him at the end of the tour to go home because I wanted to go home earlier than we did. But he's a workaholic. We're definitely two different kinds of cats, but that's what make our relationship exciting. And there's nothing wrong with a good healthy spat now and again between a bunch of Jersey Guys!   *Richie, June 1991*

Jon with Gianni Versace
and Elton John

Jon and I used to argue like crazy, it was like being married
for 10 years and after that last tour I was ready for a divorce.
He wanted to work all the time but too much work was
killing me. Physically I was a wreck. I was drinking far too
much and I was ready for the funny farm. But we spent a day
in Jersey drinking Tequila for eight hours and sorted it all
out. Macho, huh?

Richie, October 1991

We haven't ever gotten along better. People's personal
lives are light years beyond where they were three years
ago, up to six years ago. Tico and Al' and Richie are just
unfuckin'believable.

Jon at the beginning of 'Keep The Faith' tour,
September 1993

I think it's benevolent dictatorship! Everybody's opinions
are going to be considered. I think when somebody has a
vision of what they want something to be, not everybody
can have the same vision or any vision. It doesn't mean that
the guys don't support it, but I don't think Bill Wyman got as
involved as Keith or Mick in picking out the singles' bag art,
you know? So I don't think it's any slight to Alec, but
sometimes he couldn't care less about the artwork. Al is
more into, 'Hey! Why don't we learn this old cover?'

Jon, September 1993

Richie lives just down the block. I call him up to go out on
his boat – if I can get him out of bed! We had a week off
before Germany. Everyone came over to my place twice. I
went over to Dave's house for dinner one night.

Jon, September 1993

All we have really is each other, and everybody's
immediate old friends. The thing is, that the band is my
name, yes. I am the quarter-back of the team, probably
because I am the primary writer and it was my record deal
– but when I had the opportunity to go tour with Kenny
Aaronoff and we coulda asked Jeff Beck and Elton John

and all those guys – I had no desire to do that because there's a big difference between playing with great musicians and playing with a great band.

Jon, September 1993

Change is change and there's nothing you can do about it, but it is a major blow to lose one of the original members. We just have to accept it. I have nothing but the best to say about Alec, and I hope he's happy. Just because I want to constantly tour and make records doesn't mean he should have to feel like that too.   *Jon, January 1994*

It's true that Alec started to leave the band some time ago, but his commitment to recording has never been under suspicion. If ever Bon Jovi get into the rock'n'roll hall of fame, I hope Alec will be up there with us.

Jon, January 1994

We're not gonna say that so-and-so is in the band, and then have to fire him six months later. Whoever gets this gig will really have to earn his wings. He'll be filling shoes that are very difficult to fill.   *Jon, January 1994*

We've sorted out all of our differences now. Straightened all that shit out. In the end, Jon and I went on holiday together and just started writing. That's when we came up with 'Always'. I never thought we would actually break up. Never. No matter what shit we went through, I never, never thought we would ever stop. Then, when the time started slipping by and we still weren't getting it together, I always thought we would still have to get back together some day and finish this. Because it's not finished. Not yet, man, not yet.   *Richie, November 1994*

Alec was not pushed. I don't want to speak on behalf of him but there just comes a time when you don't feel like your lives are going the same way. Bon Jovi's not a life sentence, for any of us, and I'm still friends with Alec.

Jon, December 1994

We've never had a physical altercation. That these guys believed in Bon Jovi the way I believed in it, and give me the opportunity to guide it the way I see fit... I'll be forever indebted to them for that.   *Jon, February 1995*

I think everyone's pretty happy in this band. I might just be less guarded than some of them. As long as you're in a process of evolution, you're really happy. I've started to really find myself as an artist, and the band doing so well again is cool. Plus I'm married now, and it's wonderful. Heather's great, so what the fuck's not to be happy about?

Richie, February 1995

We have never stopped fun. I've never ever thought that Jon wasn't there for me. He has a good heart.

Richie, March 1995

Richie is very out-going, very happy-go-lucky. He's always got a smile for everybody. It's pretty hard not to like him. He's the kind of guy you can count on.   *Jon, March 1995*

Alec has left the band unfortunately. He left virtually after the Cross Road period when we were just starting to record These Days. He's not on the new record at all, and so we've got a guy called Hugh McDonald from New York City. Bon Jovi has always been a hard-working band and sadly Alec didn't want to work as hard any more. If we're not recording, we're touring; if we're not touring, we're making a video; if we're not making a video we're doing press. We're the kind of band that never stops, and that's why Alec flew the coop.   *Richie, June 1995*

Hugh's a very proficient studio musician who's been on about 125 records, and he also was the bass player on the song 'Runaway' before the band was formed. And the first session I ever did, back when I was 18 or so, had Hugh on bass as well, so he's sort of been around us for a while – and he just seemed to slot right in.   *Richie, June 1995*

The Keep The Faith thing was a triumph because we were just coming out of that period. The problem was we weren't really communicating at that point. He was doing his solo album. I was doing mine and we never seemed to

tie up. I don't think there was ever any real danger of us splitting, it was just a question of when we'd get together again. In my heart I always knew that the band would survive because no one ever said, 'Fuck you, this band stinks and I'm out of here.' It's just that we were together – literally – for the eight years preceding that time.

We were the kind of band that holidays together – we were disgusting! We were in each other's faces all the time for eight years, and when you're that successful that you do two 16-month tours back to back, you find yourself desperate for your own space, which is what the solo albums did for us. *Richie, June 1995*

We know each other better than brothers because we've been together for 12 years. I only wish everybody in their lives could have friends like this. It's not a relationship where it's separate dressing rooms. I couldn't handle that. Show number four would be the end of the tour and we'd be at home watching TV. *Jon, July 1995*

We argue fairly often. Most times we argue pretty logically. It's really more like a debate than anything else. When you've been together for a long time like we have, you get more relaxed in dealing with each other. *Richie, February 1996*

We got a divorce, Tico and I. Official. We're The Odd Couple. He broke me in. I was 21 and he was 10 years older than me. He'd been doing it a long time, I was bright green. We were rooming together, and I thought, 'This guy's partying so much, he's out of his fucking mind!' And I said, 'Okay, if you can't beat 'em, join 'em'.' And I almost died! We got separate rooms. *David, July 1996*

FAME – NO BED OF ROSES

People often ask if you lose a lot of friends once you become famous but I actually have very few friends and if they're good friends then they'll stand by you whether you are rich or famous or poor and unknown. I get some friends who ask me for money... funny thing is if you ask them to do some work on your house they'll charge you twice as much.

I also have a lot of trouble getting insurance for my house. They think we're wild rock'n'rollers and you'll get hurt or come home and wreck the place. My broker told me I was having more trouble than the Senator of the State.   *Tico, November 1987*

One of the big drawbacks is all the travelling. It can get very tiring, especially if you have travelled halfway across the world and have to get onstage and do the gig a couple of hours later. I guess we spend about half our time travelling and the other half looking for good-looking women. It's a tough job.   *David, November 1987*

It would be nice at times to maybe slow down and take a little bit of it in. A while ago we were getting presented with a gold disc and some of it kinda sank in and I felt real good but otherwise it's go go go.   *Alec, November 1987*

on with Eddie Murphy

The best part for me is just being up on that stage. There's times when you just feel you can't do it. Y'know like it's your 230th show that year – I read a book about someone who'd done 160 shows and I see Tina Turner on the cover of Billboard, she's done 97 shows. I laugh, I say both of them together do what I do and they're saying, 'I'm exhausted.' Oh, yeah? Tell me about it. And I get up to the back of the stage minutes before we go on and I might still be moping. But the minute I hear that crowd I just get up there man, and go nuts. I'm Sugar Ray Leonard, Jagger, Bruce, Eddie Murphy... I'm fucking Superman.
                                          Jon, November 1987

This work I do isn't real work. It's a privilege, it's a dream. Work is what my dad does – cutting hair, or like my mom does – selling brooms so she could buy me my first guitar. This is a dream and I'm just hoping I don't wake up.
                                          Jon, November 1987

I don't want to talk about my feelings on religion. Or politics. I don't think any of my fans care. It's not my place. People shouldn't want to know my opinions on religion, I'm an entertainer. *Jon, 1988*

I got this sweatshirt for free. A kid threw it over my gate and it's one of my favourites now. I also got these sneakers for free. That's one thing about having money – you suddenly get everything free. When you have no money and you're freezing in your old sneakers no ones give you shit for free. But I don't think we've become extravagant. I still wake up in the morning and thank God that I'm able to pay my hotel bill.

It's great to be about to go out to dinner and pick up the bill if you want. It's a real good feeling to know that you can go buy your old man a Mercedes every day if you want. I bought my old man a car recently, that was good. *Jon, January 1989*

It was a real problem for my parents to accept presents at first and I just couldn't understand it. But they begun to accept it for what it is now and I have as well. To me it's as much their money as mine. They're part of this. I understand how some parents get kind of strange about it. It's still not easy. I'm taking them to Italy for the first time soon but I had to give them the tickets last Christmas so they had a year to get used to the idea and accept that they don't have to go to work for a week. They both work full-time still and they can't stop working. I told them, I'll buy the god-damn businesses you work in if you'll just stop. But they don't listen. They just tell me to shut up and remember where I come from. *Jon, January 1989*

As a kid I never had first place in the race, never was the all-star baseball guy. I was always the schlep who hung in by the skin of his teeth. I just wanted to be in a rock'n'roll band. The success is a great feeling. It's not so much of a Fuck You thing but it's rewarding and the pay is really just the icing on the cake. *Jon, January 1989*

We could blow this real easy but I don't think we're that stupid. There's been an excess of people who have sold as many albums as we have and had 18 minders and had to have flower petals thrown on the ground wherever they walked, and I've sat with those people for two hours while they've told me how they screwed up. *Jon, January 1989*

I take the attitude that if the drum technician didn't show up today then I couldn't go to work. My crew has a hard time swallowing that. Because they treat me like, Oh Hosanna. I go, Ah c'mon you assholes, if any of you has a hangover today. I'm the one who is gonna suffer! I get the bad fucking review. *Jon, January 1989*

For a time you think you're more than a real person. But it wasn't really because of the way we were, it was because we were meeting these other bands and they had this superior air about them and we wanted to be like them. Then we realised these guys were stupid fuckers and we decided that if we were to get on we'd just have to be ourselves.   *Jon, January 1989*

It's not pressure, really. Deep down I think we love it. We say it's a pressure and all that shit but it's a pretty good feeling. Better than being fucking ignored, and we've had plenty of that too!   *Jon, January 1989*

In Australia, because the hotel was like, under siege, I bought this baseball cap with a wig that hangs out the bottom, real black and curly – like Harpo Marx – and I bought a little moustache. I put them on with this pair of regular eye glasses and I went into the show and I walked right past the wardrobe girl who's been with me for a year and a half and said, 'Hi, my name's Sal.' She goes, 'Hi Sal!' and kept walking. I thought, 'This is great!' Then I walked up onstage and kicked my guitar and my guitar roadie came running out and went nuts at me – 'Who the fuck do you think you are, do you know whose guitar that is?' Then I just took off the hat and peeled off the moustache real slow and stood there smiling. Man they were dying!

Then I put them back on and walked out on the street and I swear to God as soon as I got out there, the first person I walked past said, 'Hi Jon!' I couldn't believe it.
                                        Jon, January 1989

We've sold a lot of records and there's not that many teenage girls. Sure, the girls make up a big part of the audience, but their boyfriends or big brothers aren't ashamed to dig it. I'm not a little girl so I can't tell you what they like about us. *Jon, April 1989*

The greatest misconception of us is that we live in a fishbowl, that we don't go out to clubs or bars. That's wrong, because if you think that you're the guy on TV, you're finished. I think that Michael Jackson or Presley or Springsteen could, if they'd wanted to, have gone anywhere. Any time you think that because you play guitar in a rock band that you're anything more than the guy in the front row, you lose. It's bullshit. *Jon, April 1989*

Fame doesn't suck, you know. There's a lot of stuff that goes with it that I'm not comfortable with but where I come from if you're vain enough to believe that shit you get your ass kicked. And as for being rich, well that doesn't suck, bud. It doesn't suck at all. *Jon, 1989*

One of the greatest things that happened to me was when Brian May grabbed me by the arm at Wembley last year. I guess he saw a page out of his own life or whatever, but he said, 'Slow down for a second and enjoy what you guys are living because when it's all over and you've only got the memories, you're gonna go, Fuck!' He said Queen did all this stuff but they were always thinking about the next album, the next tour and they can't remember it, they went through it with blinkers on. And that's where we stand right now. *Jon, December 1989*

I know bands who play the Meadowlands in New Jersey which is a beautiful great arena and they can't really sell it out so they put up a curtain and play to half of it. Well, as a kid that was never my idea of being in a rock band, to play to half an arena. The sound of empty seats is not one I care to hear. Do you want it all or do you want half of it? It's just a simple question. Do you want great sex or do you wanna get jerked off and go home. That's basically what it becomes. Don't do it if you can't do it right. *Jon, December 1989*

My grandfather was a plumber until it killed him, believe it or not. Being a fucking plumber shouldn't kill you. My father cut hair and would've died cutting hair if I hadn't convinced him he didn't have to. That's what the world does to you; you grow up. You get a job, you get married, you have two point two children, a white picket fence, you watch TV at night and go to work five days a week. That's what the real world's all about and I wasn't ready for all that. *Jon, December 1989*

I'm not committed enough. I'm not like Michael Jackson or Madonna or the other big guys. You know the Pacinos and De Niros of this world live, eat and shit their craft. I'd just as soon go to the arena tonight, give it every single bit of everything I have and then, when it's done, go to the bar, have a couple of cold ones and go out and see the nightlife. Whereas Michael Jackson, I met him in a hotel in Japan, and I heard that after his shows he goes back to his hotel-room and sings and dances for three hours. I don't need to do that every night.

Madonna looks like she's carved out of stone, this girl's in amazing shape, she's really got it together and that's great. I'm just in a big bar band that has a great time touring. If I was really committed I'd come on looking like Adonis, singing my ass off, playing guitar better than Jeff Beck. I'm only human, I'm just being lazy. I'm admitting stupidity and, I guess, fault.
Jon, December 1989

I take my music very seriously, but people think it's more than it is. To me music is just entertainment, it's a way of getting someone in their automobile from work to home and home to work, it's the shit that comes out the speaker in an elevator. I worked my whole life on it but all it is is a way of getting a guy from the ground floor to the third without getting claustrophobic. It's entertainment. I don't wanna save the world with it. I have more respect for what Gorbachev is doing pulling down the walls than I have for Bob Dylan who was one of the geniuses. I did Dylan, but Gorbachev is trying to save the world. Now that's important.
Jon, December 1989

With Sheryl Crow

When I look back there's nothing I miss from those early days. It was hard work back then, but you've got to realise that the position occupied both by myself personally and also by the band means that it's like every day is Christmas. I haven't been in a position to regret anything. It's been a constant upward move. I'm still at a stage in my life where it's a romantic thought to try and conquer the world with your friends.

Jon, January 1990

I went to my high school reunion party the other day and I was shaking because I was so nervous. I walked in an hour late and the DJ said, Jon Bon Jovi is here! I felt such an asshole. I'm really no-one special, I'm just an ordinary guy who, the next day, went to the Meadowlands Grand Prix, bought a ticket, sat in the stands and spent the day spotting famous people. It was like, 'Wow – there's Paul Newman! Wow – there's Bill Cosby.' I had a blast.

Jon, September 1990

There are guys in every local bar in the world who can sing better than me, play better than me, are nicer guys than me and can probably kick my ass every night of the week.

Jon, September 1990

All I do know is that my life is like one big wet dream. The only thing that bothers me is that so many wonderful things happen to me that I probably won't remember half of them. But as a job I recommend it highly; it beats shovelling dirt and it sure as hell beats sitting at home. I would do it for free. In fact, if people didn't pay me to do it, I would pay them to come along and see me!

Jon, September 1990

I don't pay attention to that fame stuff. Where I'm from people don't let you act the rock star. It's very working-class and no one really gives a shit. I tested the famous waters in '85, the movie star girlfriend, the big parties, but I didn't like it, it wasn't me. I did the Young Guns record in Hollywood so I hired a house in the Hollywood Hills. I called the place Disgraceland because it was the sort of place Elvis would have loved. It was fucking tacky. It was the ugliest house in the world. The guy who owned it had thousands of dollars' worth of this ugly art up on the walls so I bought a load of Elvis posters and stuck them up over the pictures. But, I'll tell you, I could never move to Hollywood because it is Babylon. Keep me away from there.

Jon, January 1991

Well, hey, I'm in London. I'm going to try my best to get drunk tonight, to get laid tonight and steal as much money from my record company as I can. Then I'll be gone before anyone knows what the fuck happened. And tomorrow night I'm going to try it again in Sweden. Then Rome…

Jon, January 1991

Oh, I'm a romantic. Absolutely. There's nothing wrong with that. Innocence and romanticism. Let's face it, this is an ugly world. A shitty place to be. It's a bunch of whores. I'm 28, I've lived the life of 10 men already and I'm becoming cynical but I try to hold on to my romanticism. A few friends, family, songs, a couple of beers. Don't look to me to write the song about the ozone layer. I'm afraid enough about it but I'm not the guy for the job.

Jon, January 1991

To be honest, our longevity is more a result of persistence than clever forward-thinking. We just looked at everyone and said, 'Fuck off, we're still gonna be here next year – and the year after that, and if you don't like our new record then fuck it, we'll make another!' *Jon, January 1994*

It would be nice to think that we've never repeated ourselves due to artistic integrity, but the truth is that just as you change as a person, your musical tastes change, and so your writing has to change. *Jon, January 1994*

The biggest myth about fame is that it's wonderful; that it's 24-hours a day, seven days a week of parties, no pressures, and you're never lonely. That's a great misconception. *Jon, May 1994*

You could look at what we do as being like travelling salesmen. We're out on the road hawking our wares. But the more romantic way of looking at it is to think of it like being a cowboy. You ride into a town, you don't know where you are, or know where you'll sleep tonight, but you'll sleep somewhere. Tomorrow you'll get up and go somewhere else. It's awfully clichéd, but somewhat true.

Jon, September 1994

We really did run the stupidity gamut. It was like nothing you ever imagined or dreamed of, and there's nothing that can prepare you for it, and when I see a band going through it now, you feel bad for 'em, because if anything, 'Slippery...' should've been the best time of my life. But it wasn't. Things either happened too quickly or else I was physically exhausted trying to keep up with it all... I just wanted to crawl into bed and die.   *Jon, November 1994*

I went out and bought Ferraris and Mercedes for presents, and houses, and did all the stupid groupie stuff. I moved to Malibu. There were bouts of alcoholism and drugs, dope, certainly a lot of bad money blown. We got to enjoy the last hump of wild abandoned fucking, and drugs and drinking, and tour buses. I remember reading a magazine on the bus in 1985, going 'What's this thing AIDS?'   *Jon, November 1994*

My trouble is, I don't stop to smell the coffee. Richie's at home in California with the most beautiful woman in Hollywood, and I'm working a 16-hour day, every day, three different projects at the same time. And that's when I'm happiest, that's when I realise I'm a psychopath. I should be a little more like Richie, he should be a little more like me. He can miss his flight to lay in bed one more time with his girlfriend, and I'm at the airport banging on the plane to open the door. Who's sicker?   *Jon, November 1994*

These days, I don't just have the success of the band. I have Stephanie, the stability of my family life in general, and the band are all happy. The accomplishment and the challenge that exists for further accomplishment is cool.
       Jon, December 1994

Yeah, success can drive you down sometimes. It's a life force when you first pick up a guitar and get that rush, that aspiration to take on the world and conquer it. There's no greater feeling for me than to write songs that people like; but when the machine comes down and tries to eat you up, it can kill you. Even if you survive, it can still fuck you up! In rock'n'roll, you can get a lobotomy without realising what's happening! People have had the life and soul sucked out of them. It does happen.
       Jon, December 1994

As a writer, it's very satisfying to hear that what I do has had such an effect on people. That, to me, was the ultimate goal. It all came home to me recently when I met this guy who plays quarter-back for the New England Patriots. I felt like a little kid waiting to meet him, but to my amazement it turned out that he was massive Bon Jovi fan! I was nervous about meeting him, so it felt really weird for me to give him my autograph. Suddenly, it started to make sense. The quarter-back was only 21 years old, and every young person has heroes.

Jon, December 1994

I don't appreciate people banging on my door night and day. I feel that my home is the one place that should be off-limits. Otherwise, I'm always flattered that certain people care enough about the band to wanna hang out for us. I haven't forgotten what it's like to be a fan.

Jon, December 1994

There have been a couple of kooky situations, but you can't let it rule your life. This guy turned up at my door once claiming he was a messenger from Jesus! He knocks on my door with this big, greasy bag in his hand, and this evil look in his eye. And I'm so fucking dumb that I open the door! He says, 'Jon, Jesus told me to come to you! The voices won't leave me alone, man!'

But y'know what? I sat down with this guy and sorted him out. I said 'It's okay, Jesus didn't really tell you to come here. What can I do for you?' After that, he seemed totally together and felt kinda bad about it all. I didn't feel in any danger. I only pray that no one ever messes with my kid. I know my wife can take care of herself.

Jon, December 1994

At the end of the day I still enjoy the things I enjoyed 15 years ago, going to the movies, all that kinda stuff. But yeah, every day I think how lucky I am. I couldn't have made up lies like this. *Jon, January 1995*

This business can give you a big ego if you're stupid enough to let it but I'm not a prisoner of rock'n'roll, and I don't live an extravagant life. *Jon, January 1995*

With Booker T. And Eric Burdon

Ask any one of those kids outside who I was out running with today. It was me and my two feet. There has never been and there is not an army of people looking after Jon Bon Jovi, no way. I keep it really tight. Why do I need all these people? Do I need people to sit around and wipe my nose? What the fuck is that about?   *Jon, January 1995*

Fidelity isn't difficult in my line of work, not at all. The idea of fans throwing themselves at you is a fallacy.
        Jon, January 1995

Cobain's suicide really beat me up plenty, because I felt for him. But I felt more for his daughter. Having a daughter the same age, I couldn't imagine doing anything to hurt her. That really bummed me out, because if fame is too much for you, as he said – quit. You don't have to do it. You can always write songs and play in a bar in Seattle. You don't have to be in this game. So that part of it I don't get.
        Jon, February 1995

I remember the excitement of buying a ticket for a show. That ticket might be sitting in your bedroom for months while you waited for it to happen. The anticipation of going to the arena, waiting for the house lights to go up. And you as a band have to live up to those expectations.
        Jon, February 1995

We're just tickled at everything; everyone here is just pinching each other, grinning stupidly; we can't believe we're still doing it.   *Richie, June 1995*

What's most important is that I make music I care about. If I care, that's all that matters. If people care above and beyond that, I'm thankful to each and every one of them. And to everyone who keeps my organisation going. But I don't do it for any other reason because I couldn't care less at this point. Who cares when you have no money – you don't know what money is. And when you have money, who cares what money is? So it's not the money that's the motivation factor, it's simply that I make music that I enjoy making.   *Jon, September 1995*

Success does breed contempt, paranoia and a whole new set of problems that you weren't accustomed to in your life. But you have to get over them, and then you get back to what it was that moved you in the first place. As long as you can do that, there's no reason why you can't go on forever.   *Jon, November 1995*

We handle ourselves in this band – although of course the record company do things for us, but that's their job. But 'yes men' don't exist in my organisation any more. I've got

roadies who tell me I suck all the time. My monitor man goes, 'You getting paid tonight? What the fuck's your problem?' That happens plenty around here.

Jon, November 1995

Nowadays, seeing my face on a magazine cover isn't such a big deal. I don't need a pat on the back from the neighbours, the postman or the family. That's not really what it's about now. *Jon, November 1995*

Money affords you great comfort. I can pay the rent, and to me that's the greatest thing. You can see I'm not exactly the most flamboyant guy, with diamond wrist watches and all that. I don't stay in hotel suites, either. I get a regular room like everyone else. *Jon, November 1995*

I got the plane for one reason. We've flown private for eight years, and I'm never going back on that bus again. Fuck that – I'm an impatient man! If you ever see me on a bus again, you know the band's finished. It won't be any of this 'getting back to roots' shit – it'll be over!

Jon, November 1995

Life is never boring. I supposed you could say I'm a lunatic workaholic, but that's what gets me up in the morning.

Jon, January 1996

It's a good job if you can get it you know. It was the rainbow at the end of all my dreams. When I think about all the things that we've accomplished in our lifetimes, all the things I've seen and places we've been, it's incredible.

Jon, March 1996

I get a bigger thrill out of writing a song than I do recording it or performing it live, because that feeling of doing it is going to be with you forever. That's probably the real reason why I'll carry on doing this, because I don't know that I'd necessarily get a hard-on over the idea of packing up a suitcase all over again. We've done too many of those kinds of tours where it's got too much. This summer we're only doing 30 shows and I know we could have done another 50 but that's out of the question. I want it to be relaxed and 30 shows is like a fun vacation.

Jon, March 1996

But I want you to know, I don't need this. Most definitely, life would still be worth living if I couldn't do this. Whenever I had a job in an auto parts store or a fast food restaurant, I was happy. I was comfortable. In the town I came from, you had a paint factory or a brick making factory or you joined the navy and that was how people got out. I just got out a different way. *Jon, May 1996*

When I hear about Oasis throwing TVs out of windows and buying Rolls Royces I laugh, because we did it. Everybody did it. Keith Richards did it, and John Lennon before that. All the stuff about, 'We're the young band, we're going grab girls' tits on a TV show', we've all done it and that's what it's all about when you get out there.

Jon, March 1996

I got the Superman tattoo on my arm after Slippery... came out, because I felt superhuman. I had an album selling a million a month. I was on the cover of Rolling Stone. I was so inconceivable, it was funny to us.

Jon, May 1996

It's a funny feeling. I don't feel old, but in the same breath I feel like an elder statesman. You know what I mean?

Jon, June 1996

In America, the song 'Keep The Faith' woke us up by not doing so well. We ran into a brick wall, because we'd gotten used to the success of Slippery When Wet and New Jersey. Even my solo album, Blaze Of Glory, was big! I really believed that 'Keep The Faith' was a great song and it was gonna work, but when it didn't it made us hungry, humble and focused.

Jon, June 1996

When we were younger, the lifestyle of sex, drugs and rock and roll applied to this band in full force. If you want to talk about percentages, let's talk about 100,000 per cent! We really had a good time. There wasn't a lot of sleeping going on in my room for the early years of this organisation. During our rocky period, the New Jersey tour of '88, we were so fucked up we didn't remember a lot of the cool things we did. But I don't think our shows

suffered. Quite honestly, I don't think Bon Jovi's ever had any bad shows.   *Richie, July 1996*

I thank God before I go on stage. I just go, 'Thank you for letting me do this, it's really cool!' I still get freaked out. How many people get a chance to walk out in front of a stadium crowd and play one of their songs and have 80,000 people get right into it? It's a very special feeling. It's a privilege.   *Richie, July 1996*

Vanity aside, we're one of the best rock bands I've seen. Hey, we're good!   *Jon, July 1996*

I may have talked about pussy, I may even have chased it. But it's highly unlikely I would have followed through – I can't swear to it because I can't remember those times. Back then the bond I had with my wife was the only thing remaining consistent in my life. She stopped me jumping out of a moving car one time.   *Jon, August 1996*

We went to do this MTV awards show. They were giving us a lifetime achievement award. What had we done? Four miserable albums and we weren't getting along. I realised that all we were there for was to help the ratings. So we show up and I won't sit with them, they won't sit with me. I get loaded. I collect the prize, walk off stage and give it away to a girl I knew. In the limo afterwards, the manager said, 'There should be some changes round here.' I said, 'Great idea!' And I fired him.   *Jon, August 1996*

Rock'n'roll's been a life-consuming project for me for over 10 years now – the music, the women, the drinking. Rock'n'roll is a lifestyle. It's something that's with you when you wake up in the morning, and when you go to sleep it's still there. You kind of wear it, like a coat. It's like a cloak, man; it's your colours.   *Richie*

HOMEWARD BOUND

My wife left me because of the band and everything. But fuck it, I'd have left the bitch anyway. There's only a certain amount you can do on the telephone and believe me I've tried everything. But one of the big problems about being in a big band is when you go home, which I've done once or twice in the last four years, you suddenly have all this 'family' that you never knew existed and surprise, surprise they're all down on their luck and need a few bucks. These are very often people you have never even heard of, let alone seen before.   *Alec, November 1987*

We went out and got very drunk in Las Vegas, went to a tattoo parlour and got myself a new tattoo, went gambling in a casino, won lots and lots of money and I said 'Hey! Let's get married!' So we went and we did that and then we got back to the hotel before the bar closed. We didn't have a best man, nothing. Nobody knew. I didn't tell anyone. I didn't take anyone. I tell you, I got a tattoo, I got drink, I won money and I got married. Next day I woke up and said, 'I did what?'   *Jon, August 1989*

Las Vegas. Hell. Polyester hell. That's a good way to put that fucking miserable town. I got married there. I was so fucking on top of the world that day. I'd played two shows at the LA Forum, and every poseur in LA came there with their arms folded and said, 'Impress me' and the gigs were so great and I brought Little Richard out of retirement, I had a billboard of my band in Sunset Strip, I had the Number One record in America and I got a new tattoo, and I was looking for something to do that night. I was gonna go out and be a poseur in LA and get my picture taken, which I never ever do…

I was full of shit and I was running off to get married. I had to be on a plane in an hour. She Dorothea said no. I said 'It's now or never'. And after all these years, she knew that never meant never. I just can't believe it, but we made the plane. The ceremony was over in five minutes. We used two plastic rings. When she put it on my finger, it broke, shattered in a hundred pieces. I'll never wear a ring again because of that. We were back in LA before the bar closed, and we had a drink and went to bed. It was a long day. What a day.   *Jon, September 1989*

If I'm onstage when that call comes I'll be out of there and on the first Concorde flight home. I speak to my wife, Dorothea, every day. This is the most important thing in the

Jon and Dorothea

world for us, and I'll be dropping anything and everything to get back there for the birth. If I'm onstage the rest of the band can carry on without me. *Jon, May 1993*

I could be having a miserable day, worrying about the business, the group, playing, writing music – but then I'd look at Dorothea and go, 'I don't give a damn about that.' And you realise that having a family is so much more important. *Jon, April 1995*

David, my keyboard player, just had twins. So there'll be four kids on the next tour! *Jon, April 1995*

Jesse's only two months old and he needs to see my face and hear my voice. Stephanie looks at aeroplanes and says 'There's daddy'. That's tough to take. Instead of being on a pony in our backyard, she's going to spend her second birthday somewhere in Germany. *Jon, July 1995*

Dorothea is my best friend. She always been there for me, in the ups and downs, and she gave me my kids. *Jon, September 1995*

My life has changed dramatically since I became a dad. When I'm not touring, I'm up at seven in the morning and I go to bed a lot earlier and like taking naps. There isn't

Dorothea and Stephanie

Jon and Dorothea

music all the time in my house any more, or me sitting at the piano at two in the morning. Those days are gone.

Jon, September 1995

As a father you see there's more to life than just you, which is so important. You grow and grow up. Everyday is a new bond. I can see why people have tons of kids because they're just the best. *Jon, September 1995*

Each time we went for it, it happened. My wife refers to me as the King! *Jon, September 1995*

Who would I die for? My kids, my wife, my parents. I'm somewhat over-romantic, but I would die for truth, for loyalty, and for love. *Jon, September 1995*

It was unbelievable. You think you love somebody until you have kids, then you really learn what love is. You can't fully understand the feelings before it happens to you. When you're sitting through labour and the baby comes – Wow! Tears. Help me! Oh Christmas! – it changes you forever. *Jon, September 1995*

Kids have made me a lot calmer. Patience develops with time and I didn't have it at first. When Stephanie was a baby and crying, I didn't know what to do with her.

Jon, September 1995

I've learnt much more about London. Stephanie is in nursery school and we walk her there. Both in Rumsen and in Malibu where we have houses, you can't walk anywhere. That is the biggest thing that I love about this. We go out of our door, we walk five minutes and we're at a pub or a restaurant. That's really exciting. Yesterday we went to a premier of a cartoon for kids. We took two of the neighbour's kids too, and that's the first time I've done that. I've never worked out in a gym in my life, but there's a cool gym I can go to where the people are great. I'm really enjoying living in London. *Jon, March 1996*

It's not that we're getting softer, or that I'm writing baby songs, but it's difficult in the morning when my daughter comes in and goes 'Put a shirt on' or 'You better shave' to relate to that other stuff. The kids are so young that I'm not going to miss any of that. I don't want to do 240 shows a year. I don't want to be anybody's machine. I want to love every night that I'm up there. *Jon, March 1996*

I have the health of my two kids and a wife that loves me. That's the most gratifying thing. I would trade it all in a minute to guarantee the health of my kids.

Jon, March 1996

FAITH IN THE FUTURE

We're enjoying ourselves so much as a band these days that the future looks better than ever. We tried to get over the loss of our bass player and just like when grunge came in and people were worried, we've had to fight. But then something like Cross Road comes up and we carry on surviving.

As long as the music and everything stays fun, we'll carry on. We all have outside interests that keep us busy so that when we get back together it's great. In the future we just want to keep writing, keep working and on a personal note, have a happy marriage. *Richie, June 1995*

There's no official band activity for another two years. But we had dinner together recently – Dave, Richie and me. We went to a local sushi bar near Richie's place. Richie starts his record this week in LA. Dave might play on it. Dave's also getting his songwriting together, writing for a lot of different people. And I spoke to Tico the other day, and he's just opened an art gallery in Miami.

Jon, January 1996

I had a discussion with someone last week about politics. We were talking about our leaders and our Presidents being selected, and how the dream has faded. But up until John Kennedy was assassinated, Americans, and probably a lot of the world, believed that the white picket fence, two point two kids, a chicken in the pot, and a car in the garage theory was going to be true forever. Now I get really bothered that the kids are growing up in a world that says that you have no future. If you're told that long enough, you start to believe it. *Jon, March 1996*

There will be a big break before we record the next Bon Jovi album, partly because we are all doing our own thing – I'm working on the film, Richie's recording a solo album and the others all have their own projects. We've had three albums out in the past four years and we felt it's time to stop for a break.   *Jon, April 1996*

I think it's good to break for a couple of years. I got gallery shows set up, starting in October. And I give money to help kids in schools, so I get to meet young artists. It's interesting to find out where they're coming from, because we live in a shell. A lot of the time you don't get to talk to the average person.   *Tico, July 1996*

I have a hard time with organised religion. How is it that a baby can die at birth and under Catholicism he doesn't go to heaven because he has original sin until he's christened? How come if you go to confession, walk out of church and say 'God damn it' for some reason, then you get hit by a bus, no good, you go to hell? How come they won't let women be priests? You got a priest makes his vows, he's skimming money, he's sleeping with little boys. You go to mass three times a day, sing a song, put money in the plate, that's supposed to absolve you of your sins. I have a hard time with all those things.   *Jon, August 1996*